Exposition on the Cost of Capital

Exposition on the Cost of Capital

A thesis submitted to the Faculty of the University of Delaware in partial fulfillment of the requirements for the degree of Master in Business Administration

June, 1969
REVISED, 2020

BERNARDO ANTONIO MARISTANY Y COSTALES-GONZÁLEZ

MILL CITY PRESS

Mill City Press
2301 Lucien Way #415
Maitland, FL 32751
407.339.4217
www.xulonpress.com

Printed in the United States of America.

Paperback ISBN-13: 978-1-6322-1724-0
Hard Cover ISBN-13: 978-1-6322-1725-7
eBook ISBN-13: 978-1-6322-1726-4

Approved: ___Denis T. Raihall___

Professor in charge of thesis on behalf of the
Advisory Committee

Approved: ___Rulee V. Austin___

Dean of the College of Business and Economics

Approved: ___T. Kilpatrick___

Dean of the College of Graduate Studies

Acknowledgements

S everal persons have kindly helped me to conclude this work. I would be remiss if I did not mention Dr. Gordon R. Bonner, whose advice, given at just the right time, kept me working on this M.B.A. program; Dr. Denis T. Raihall who effectively guided and advised me in defining and developing this work; Mr. Alan G. Bates, who read and commented on one of the early manuscripts.

I am grateful to these and to others for their help and encouragement.

TABLE OF CONTENTS

Chapter I

Introduction

This work does not necessarily prove or disprove anything. It is an exposition of the current body of more or less accepted thinking on the subject of cost of capital. It is partly an exposition of the logic of the thinking, but it is primarily an exposition of its importance in the context of the world in which this thinking is used.

The cost of Capital is closely related to the capital investment decision. Two investment evaluation methods predominate (in the literature): The present value and the yield rate of return.

The present value P of any project is found by discounting at the appropriate rate all future net cash flows to their present value equivalent. Assume that the present investment of a sum C results in the sums $A_1, A_2,...A_n$ arising respectively at the end of years $1, 2,...n$. Given the appropriate rate of discount, r, their aggregate present values can be expressed as

$$p = \sum_{i=1}^{i=n} \frac{A_i}{(1+r)^i}$$

where Σ is the conventional symbol indicating summation of the sums A_i, from the first, Ai (indicated by $i = 1$) to the n'th,

A_n (indicated by i = n). To determine the attractiveness of any investment in these very simple conditions it is necessary merely to compare P with C.

In the case where cash flows vary annually in an irregular fashion, there is no formula to compute the present value of the series in one calculation. If there are fifteen such annual cash flows, it is necessary to execute fifteen separate discount calculations in the manner described above and add the fifteen separate present values. However, if the series of cash flows follow a regular pattern then short cut calculations can be used. Examples of such regular patterns are annuities, perpetuities, cash flows increasing or decreasing at constant rates or at compound rates.

The yield rate of return is that rate of interest which discounts the future net cash flows of a project to equality with its capital investment; that is, it is the interest rate which results in a zero net present value. In normative form, the yield rate of return is the solution r to this equation:

$$C = \sum_{i=1}^{i=n} \frac{A_i}{(1+r)^i}$$

where the symbols are as previously defined. Trial and error is the usual method to solve for the yield rate, but the basic evaluation method itself is not trial and error.

Both methods use as accept-reject criterion some interest rate. When using the present value method to evaluate an investment proposal, this interest rate is used to discount the stream of future cash incomes to a reference time, usually the present. The sum of the discounted cash incomes is then compared to the present value of the capital investments, and if the sum is larger the proposal is presumably acceptable.

When using the yield rate of return method, the computed rate of return expected from the investment proposal is compared to the mentioned interest rate. If the yield rate of return is higher, the proposal is presumably acceptable.

The interest rate being used as accept-reject criterion, in this context, is referred to as the cost of capital. Thus, the utmost importance of the cost of capital.

Chapter II, of this exposition, comments on the identification of a criterion of goodness which would permit the selection of the "best". Only after specifying the criterion of goodness is it possible to develop measuring methods and decision rules.

In broad terms, two criteria of goodness have been proposed: maximizing the utility of the existing shareholders of the firm or maximizing the utility of the entity, or firm. The first criterion is universally specified by authors in this field and the body of this work rests on it. The second criterion is described as a reasonable possibility.

Having introduced the maximization of shareholder's utility as the universally accepted criterion of goodness, Chapter III presents the traditional view: the thinking that stock prices are a function of the firm's net income and that the cost of capital is a function of the firm's capital structure.

Traditionalists hold that financial policy influences the cost of capital. If a firm uses judicious amounts of leverage its total market value would be larger than what it would be without leverage. Increasing the proportion of debt, up to a critical point, increases the expected market value of the firm. If debt increases beyond the critical point, capitalization rates rise sufficiently to offset the additional earnings of the common stock, therefore the market value of the firm declines. Traditionalists maintain that there is a wide range in which the leverage ratio may move while the cost of capital is less than what it would be without leverage.

Chapter IV expounds on the traditional view that the cost of capital is the weighted average of the cost of debt and equity.

Diverse legal instruments and contractual variations characterize the acquisition of debt capital, but the whole process might be reduced to determining an interest rate. The magnitude of the cost of capital would be affected by the interest rate on debt and by the proportion of debt in the capital structure.

The cost of equity would be the capitalization rate of shareholders, the interest rate at which expected gains equal the present sum invested. Two schools of thought are defined with respect to what determines the capitalization rate: one, that it is determined by the dividends, the other, that it is determined by retained earnings. Recently it has been shown that these two approaches are, in fact, equivalent.

Chapter V considers the thinking that stock prices are a function of operating income and that the cost of capital is independent of the firm's financial structure.

The Modigliani-Miller Hypothesis is the best exponent of this thinking, therefore, this chapter presents it in some detail. Emphasis is placed on their first proposition and its premises.

Their first proposition states that in equilibrium, the market value of any firm is independent of its capital structure and is given by capitalizing its expected return at a rate appropriate to its class. The main premise on which this proposition rests is that personal leverage, through arbitrage operations, is an adequate and efficient substitute for corporate leverage.

Personal leverage consists in that the investor buys unlevered securities of firm A by borrowing for his personal account instead of buying securities of the levered firm B, both firms in an equivalent return class. An equivalent return class defines a homogeneous group of firms. It may be contrasted with the traditional industrial classifications. In this latter, the homogenizing factor is the commodity produced. In the equivalent return class the homogenizing factor is that the return on shares issued by any firm in any given class is proportional to the return of the shares issued by any other firm in the same class. Therefore, in a perfect capital market in equilibrium, the market value per dollar's worth of expected return is the same for all shares of a given class.

Chapter VI contrasts the main conclusions of the traditional and the Modigliani-Miller hypotheses and presents other approaches. R. L. Carson, as well as A. A. Robicheck and S. C. Myers, take issue with the Modigliani- Miller view that the cost of capital is independent of investment financing.

A. J. Boness attempts to conciliate both hypotheses by interpreting the financial risk in the Modigliani-Miller argument as the risk undertaken by a lender that his loan may be defaulted. Thus, he distinguishes between implicit and explicit rates. The implicit rate required when no risk of default exists, the explicit rate required when risk by default exists. The difference between both rates being a risk premium dependent only on the proposed project. Boness derives a weighted average cost of capital formulation where the interest on debt is the implicit rate. Then, he transforms Modigliani and Miller's second proposition into the same form, thus concluding that they are equivalent.

E. M. Lerner and W. T. Carleton are developing a new approach to the problem of maximizing common shares present value. In general, the problem has been approached with one equation having one independent variable and one dependent variable, all else assumed given. They propose instead to use multiple equation models to handle multiple unknowns simultaneously. Their model is narrowly limited and their hypothesis is at a relatively early stage of development.

Chapter VII describes in some detail the approach developed by W. J. Baumol and B. G. Malkiel. They do not attack the work of Modigliani and Miller, but rather build on it by adding the effect of taxes and transaction costs. They show that an optimal capital structure does exist; that the firm should borrow the maximum consistent with prudence and legal or institutional limitations; that dividend policy is relevant to the shareholder and that personal leverage is not an efficient substitute for corporate leverage.

Baumol and Malkiel, like Modigliani and Miller, attempt to conciliate an apparent contradiction between financial theory and economic analysis. On standard economic theory, the real cost of homogeneous resources is the cost of the cheapest resource available. In corporate finance, the cost of capital is a weighted average of the cost of capital from all resources available.

These authors agree that these propositions of economic theory and corporation finance are not really conflictive because they apply to different matters. They claim that the interest rate on debt and the expected yield on equity are only nominal costs, not real costs. The debt interest rate understates the true cost of debt by neglecting the leverage risk incurred by more borrowing. The expected yield on equity neglects the risk reduction resulting from lowered leverage ratio when there is an equity increase. When both debt and equity are used, neither has a real lower marginal cost, precisely as economic theory requires. But because taxes and transaction costs exist, the marginal cost of new shares may be greater than that of new debt or retained earnings.

Chapter II

The Criterion Of Goodness

The investment decision is that of choosing the best alternative investment available. The problem seems simple but it is not. The first complication is to specify a criterion of goodness which would permit the identification of the "best". If a single, unquestioned measure of "best" existed, this would not present any difficulty.

In one sense such measure exists: Best is that which maximizes utility. The utility represented by each investment alternative could be measured and compared to others, and the one maximizing utility would be chosen. However, the concept of utility is not absolute but relative to or of someone or ones. Therefore, a decision must be made according to whose utility function should be used, unless it is assumed that all parties concerned have identical utility functions. Thus, neither the present value nor the yield rate of return method can be used without first specifying the maximizing utility function.

Maximizing the Utility of Shareholders

The universal utility function specified by authors in this field is that of the existing shareholders of the firm. In other words, and assuming that money is a linear representation of utility, the investment selection criterion is that of maximizing the present value of existing shareholder's wealth. Then, the interest rate which correlates with the maximization of shareholder's wealth is called the cost of capital. The body of this work rests on this assumption, explicitly or implicitly.

Maximizing the Utility of the Entity

The investment selection criterion could be to maximize the present value of the firm's, or entity's wealth. In this context the entity is thought of as being distinct and separate from the stockholding group. This entity is difficult and perhaps impossible to define precisely. Yet, it is a useful and meaningful approximation of the nature of the modern firm.[1] [2] [3]

The large publicly held firm is an entity in itself. No one "owns" the firm. Laws exist relating to it, but they really apply in force to its much smaller brethren.

The existence of the entity might be caused by several factors: the suppliers of capital, the people who do the work and make the decisions for the entity, the people who buy and sell to the entity and most important, the society which specifies rules

---

[1] A. D. H. Kaplan, <u>Big Enterprise in a Competitive System</u> (Washington, D.C.: The Brookings Institution, 1964), p. 59.

[2] Abrams, retired chairman of the board of Standard Oil, quoted in "Have Corporations a Higher Duty than Profits?", Fortune, August 1960, p. 108.

[3] Morris, <u>The Economic Theory of Managerial Capitalism</u> (New York: The Free Press of Glencoe, 1964).

9

for the entity. Regardless of whether one speaks of the entity or of the organization, somewhere in this undefined mass, a center of authority exists which determines the direction in which the entity attempts to move. When one speaks of "management," the reference is really to the center of power.

Management, in this sense, may be the president, the board of directors or someone else. It may not be the same in all firms and is difficult to define but it exists. In this sense, management is the embodiment of the entity. The entity has no goals unless they are perceived and accepted by management.

It may happen that the goal of the firm is consistent with maximizing shareholder's wealth, but it does not follow by necessity. In this theory, the shareholder is no more than one of the prerequisites for the firm's existence. It would seem reasonable to propose that in view of the conflicting interests involved, if maximization should be a goal, it should be in terms of the entity itself. Therefore, a criterion for the investment decision would be in terms of maximizing the present value of the entity, from the viewpoint of the entity. This criterion raises the question of determining the discount rate.

Because management is the embodiment of the entity, management's preferences may be the measure of the preferences of the entity. A discount rate is an explicit statement of time preference for expected cash flows. Time preferences, in the last analysis, are very subjective, although they may be affected by quantifiable elements.

The point is that a statement by management of a required rate of return may be interpreted as an expression of the entity's time preference. This would hold regardless of how management determines the rate, or how ideas about risk have influenced this determination. This interpretation might not be worse than saying that it is an accurate measure of the time preferences of a composite of all stockholders in the firm.

This entity approach represents a violent breach of traditional thinking on this matter and is certainly not widely accepted among economists, therefore, it deserves only this brief mention in this exposition. If it were ever accepted, it would bring with it other implications.

Perhaps the most notorious implication would be that "cost of capital" would be a misnomer for the accept-reject discount rate. Similarly to the accounting entity theory, the cost of additional equity capital to the entity would be the future dividend payment. Also, the discounted rate of return would be treated as a constant.

Government also has investment decisions to make. The maximization of shareholder's wealth theory offers no help to governments. The entity approach, however, may be useful, since entity does not refer to private profit-seeking firms. In the private sector, it is customary to use the marginal efficiency of capital as the required rate of return. In contrast, the entity approach would justify an independently, although subjectively, determined rate. This rate could be higher or lower than the private sector's marginal efficiency of capital, according to the prevailing political philosophy.

Admittedly, the entity approach lacks a rigorous theory as well as a rigorous, computational solution, but its logical arguments are sufficiently strong to deserve mention.

Chapter III

The Traditional Hypothesis

David Durand[4] identified two possible approaches to the costs of debt and equity funds: one, the Net Operating Income (NOI) Method, might be considered a starting point for the Modigliani and Miller hypothesis, while the other, the Net Income (NI) Method, is essentially the traditional view. He shows that the problems of measuring capital costs are much the same as those of appraising the going concern value of a business.

The Problems of Measuring Capital Costs

Accepting the premise that businessmen seek their self-interest, which is compatible with stockholders self-interest, and that their self-interest is best served by maximizing their present worth, the measurement of the cost of capital becomes the measurement of the return required to sustain the investor's present worth. Therefore, a suitable method for common stock appraisal is needed. This method would allow us to determine whether or not a given investment would increase the investor's present

---

[4] D. Durand, "Costs of Debt and Equity Funds for Business: Trends and Problems of Measurement," <u>Conference on Research in Business Finance</u> (New York: National Bureau of Economic Research, Inc., 1952), pp. 215-247.

worth. The decision criterion would be the return required to maintain the investor's present worth.

Durand expressed the required return as:

$$RR = I + V\frac{dC}{dX}$$

where: I is the marginal rate of interest on debt

V is the "investment value" meaning the discounted value of an expected income stream

$\frac{dc}{dx}$ is the rate of change in the capitalization rate (percent) as the debt burden increases.

The equation means that the RR is equal to the rate of interest as long as the capitalization rate remains constant; but if the capitalization rate increases, the RR exceeds the rate of interest. Therefore, any practical use of the RR needs an acceptable method for estimating the behavior of the capitalization rate. Durand presented two views on the behavior of the capitalization rate.

On the single question of capitalizing earnings, these two views use fundamentally different assumptions leading to different results. Table I shows the case of a hypothetical firm, with enough data to illustrate the different views. Assume that the bonds sell in the market at par and that no taxes exist.

One view, the NOI Method, reasons that what is capitalized is net operating income because the manner in which claimants to it distribute it among themselves should not affect the total value of bonds and shares. Based on this assumption, given the common shares market price, what is the capitalization rate, or conversely, given the capitalization rate, what is the appropriate common share market price?

13

Given a common share market price of $10 per share, the capitalization rate would be estimated as follows. The total value of 1,500,000 shares of common stock is $15,000,000. The par value of bonds is $5,000,000 and the firm's total value is $20,000,000. Net operating income is $2,000,000, therefore, the rate at which net operating income is being capitalized is 10%.

The alternative view, the NI Method, capitalizes net income. Given a common share market price of $10, the capitalization rate would be estimated as follows. The total value of common stock is $15,000,000. Net income is $1,800,000, therefore, the rate at which net income is being capitalized is 12%.

TABLE I

HYPOTHETICAL BALANCE SHEET AND INCOME STATEMENT

Balance Sheet

Assets		Liabilities	
Cash	$3,000,000	Accruals	$1,000,000
Accounts Receivable	5,000,000	Accounts Payable	4,000,000
Inventory	7,000,000		
Total Current	$15,000,000	Total Current	$5,000,000
Plant and Equipment	15,000,000	Bonded Debt:	
less depreciation		4% Common	5,000,000
		stock: 1,500,000	
		shares at $10	15,000,000
		Earned Surplus	5,000,000
Total Fixed	$15,000,000	Total Fixed	$25,000,000
TOTAL	$30,000,000	TOTAL	$30,000,000

Income Statement

Sales	$30,000,000
Cost of Goods Sold	28,000,000
Net Operating Income	$2,000,000
Interest	$200,000

Conversely, given a 10% capitalization rate, the market value of a common share would be estimated as follows :

NOI Method:

Net operating income	$ 2,000,000
Capitalization rate, 10%	x 10
Total value of company	$20,000,000
Total bonded debt	5,000,000
Total value of common stock	15,000,000
Value per share, 1,500,000 shares	$10

NI Method:

Net operating income	$2,000,000
Interest	200,000
Net Income	1,800,000
Capitalization rate, 10%	x 10
Total value of common stock	$18,000,000
Value per share, 1,500,000 shares	$12

Under this method, the total investment value increases with the proportion of bonds in the capital structure, within limits. Assume three different proportions of bond financing:

Assumed amount of bonds, 4%		$2,500,000	$5,000,000
Net income	$2,000,000	1,900,000	1,800,000
Value of common stock capital-ized at 10%	20,000,000	19,000,000	18,000,000
Total investment value	20,000,000	21,500,000	23,000,000

Although the traditional hypothesis disagrees with the NOI view, it is not the NI view in pure form. It is a modified NI theory in this sense: It suggests that if a corporation uses moderate amounts of leverage, the interest on debt and the capitalization rate applied to common stock earnings do not rise to the same degree that risk premiums attached to the leverage used by individuals rise. Therefore, increasing the proportion of debt used to finance a firm would increase the expected market value of the firm up to some critical proportion of leverage. Beyond that point, capitalization rates rise sufficiently to offset the added earnings available to common stock, resulting in a decline in the market value of the firm.

The traditional hypothesis recognizes that firms live in a world of uncertainties and relies heavily on history:

> It is a basic assumption of this book that the processes of the stock market are psychological more than arithmetical. This produces the well known tendency of stock prices as a whole to go to extremes in either direction, as optimism or pessimism holds sway. In the same way, we are certain, it produces a tendency for favored stocks to sell at unduly high prices at the same time that unpopular stocks are selling at unduly low prices. This characteristic shows itself in an

extraordinarily wide dispersion of the market's capitalization rates...[5]

The preceding quotation illustrates the attitude of conservative traditionalists, whose estimates are generally based on simple algebraic relationship and much personal judgment. In recent years, traditionalists have been joined by authorities more inclined to use mathematical tools:

> In short, the thesis that a company's cost of capital is independent of its financial structure is not valid. As far as the leverage effect alone is concerned (and ignoring all the other considerations that might influence the choice between debt and equity), there does exist a clearly definable optimum position—namely, the point at which the marginal cost of more debt is equal to, or greater than, a company's average cost of capital.[6]

To traditionalists the cost of capital to the firm is the aggregate of the opportunity cost of retained earnings plus the interest paid on securities. Therefore, the cost of capital changes with the market value of the firm's securities and with the foregone

---

[5] B. Graham, D. L. Dodd, S. Cottle, and C. Tatham, Security Analysis (Fourth Edition; New York: McGraw-Hill Book Company, 1962), p. 513.

[6] E. Solomon, "Leverage and the Cost of Capital," J. of Finance, XVII (2), 1963, p. 279.

opportunities that could be taken for the best possible outside use of retained earnings.

Financial Policy and the Cost of Capital

Traditionalists maintain that the choice of financial policy definitely influences the cost of capital. They sustain that there is a range through which the greater the leverage of the firm's capital structure, the lower its capital costs. They claim that the evidence shows that investors do not believe that risk increases significantly with "judicious" leverage. Therefore, as leverage and earnings per share increase, without an offsetting increase in the capitalization rate of the shares, the price per common share would increase. It follows that the cost of capital to the firm would decrease.

The requirement of "judicious" leverage implies a limit to the acceptance by investors of the additional financial risk brought about by leverage, without demands for greater compensation, i.e., lowering the price they are willing to pay for an expected stream of future compensations. At some point investors would decide that their risk increases substantially; the capitalization rate for the equity shares starts to rise thus the cost of capital increases.

Yet, traditionalists claim that there is a wide range in which the leverage ratio may move while the cost of capital is less than what it would be without leverage. While in this range, from zero to the critical point, the firm should get needed funds by borrowing rather than by issuing equity shares.

Generally, traditionalists agree that leverage reduces the cost of capital, but some difference of opinions exists as to how much is ''judicious'' for a particular firm and as to what is "optimum" leverage. This last is the problem of deciding just when the risk from leverage becomes excessive and the cost of capital starts to rise.

The decision as to the amount of leverage to employ represents a compromise among the factors of suitability, income, risk, control, maneuverability, and timing. The compromise is reached within a certain environment, made up of the economy, the industry and the firm itself.

Traditional Rules of Thumb

Several rules of thumb have been proposed as guides to maximum leverage permissible. These rules generally indicate borrowing limits to use in financing fixed assets, or earnings limits as to how much of net income may be committed safely to fixed charges. The reason for financing fixed assets with long-term funds has to do with the cash flows obtained from the assets. A fixed asset provides services for several years. Through the use of these services a cash flow is obtained, part of which is for recovery of a portion of the investment in the fixed asset. Because of the nature of fixed assets, the recovery of the investment is a relatively slow process. Therefore, it would not be prudent to promise to pay a creditor, who has financed fixed assets, at a faster rate than we are able to obtain cash inflows from these assets.

An analogous argument militates against using long-term debt or equity to finance temporary current assets. When accounts receivable and inventory contract, it should be possible to use excess cash to repay debt. It would be unprofitable to pay interest on a loan when the borrowed funds are idle.

Consequently, there is logic in limiting long-term borrowing to a percentage of fixed assets.

One authority[7] proposes this rule of thumb: Bonds and preferred stock offerings should be limited to a maximum of one-half the tangible fixed assets value, i.e., their reproduction cost less depreciation.

One may abstract consideration of current assets in applying this rule of thumb, assuming that current assets exceed current liabilities sufficiently so that the risk of default from an excess of current liabilities is not present. This rule, like all rules of thumb, may be modified. In this case modifications may be justified by extremes in the economy or the preferences of investors. It is inapplicable where regulatory agencies prescribe certain degrees of leverage.

Earnings rules are formulated in terms of coverage of interest payments. The same authority suggests that earnings after income taxes should cover interest payments on debt by not less than three times. Standards for specific industries have developed in part from the publication of average ratios for different industries by Dun and Bradstreet, Inc., Robert Morris Associates, and others.

---

[7] H. G. Guthman, and H. E. Dougall, <u>Corporate Financial Policy</u> (Englewood Cliffs, N.J.: Prentice-Hall, Inc., 1955), pp. 217-225.

However, since leverage is commonly expressed as the ratio of debt to total capitalization, the asset rule might be emphasized here rather than the earnings rule. Then, traditionalists propose that the firm increase its leverage (decrease its cost of capital) up to the point where investors refuse to accept more risk for the same return. The maximum leverage ratio will vary with firm and industry characteristics. Yet, the rule of thumb says that a leverage ceiling of about one-half the asset value less depreciation of the tangible assets is acceptable.

These rules of thumb imply the assumption that firms within the same industry are subject to equivalent degrees of basic business or industry uncertainty, the rule of thumb aimed at the financial uncertainty. Basic business uncertainty includes all those factors, other than financing transactions, which contribute to uncertainty of the receipt of the firm's income stream. For instance, the firm's competitive position, the determinants of demand for its products and the structure of its costs. Financial uncertainty arises from the inclusion of fixed-commitment financing in the firm's capital structure.

Ronald F. Wippern[8] has examined the validity of the assumption that firms within the same industry are in an equivalent risk-class. Because the degree of variability in the earnings stream before financing charges and taxes is consistently cited as the main determinant of the amount of fixed-charge financing that may be accepted by the firm, and because the main undesirable effect of leverage seems to be that it magnifies the effects

---

[8] R. F. Wippern, "A Note on the Equivalent Risk Class Assumption," The Engineering Economist, XI (3), 1966, pp. 13-22.

of change in operating income on the income stream to stock-holders, his study uses as a proxy measure of uncertainty a measure of the variability of the firm's earnings before fixed charges and taxes.

Wippern addresses himself to these questions: Do objectively determinable risk classes exist? Do these classes correspond to industry groups?

His study includes sixty-one firms in eight industry groups. He concludes that given the validity of the proxy-uncertainty variable used, industry groups do not provide an adequate basis on which to insure homogeneity of basic business uncertainty.

Optimal Capital Structure

Eli Schwartz[9] attempted to develop a self-contained theory of the financial structure of the individual firm, suggesting that there is perhaps a single optimum capital structure, or that at least, the range of rational capital structures is narrowly bounded. By "financial structure" he means the total of all liabilities and ownership claims, the sum of the credit side of the balance sheet. His basic operating assumptions are: that the optimum capital structure for any publicly held firm is one which maximizes the long-run value per share of the common stock on the market; and that individual firms face two types of risks: external and internal.

---

[9] E. Schwartz, "Theory of the Capital Structure of the Firm," J. of Finance, XIV (1), 1959, pp. 18-39.

The external risk is a composite of the stability of earnings, liquidity, safety and marketability of the firm's assets. The internal risk is the financial risk of the firm's capital structure, and is set by the types of liabilities and the amounts carried in proportion to equity capital.

Schwartz's perception with regards to an optimum capital structure may be illustrated as follows. Assume three firms, A, B, C, in the same industry and of about the same size. Firm A is unlevered, earns about $2.00 per share. Firm B has some moderate leverage and earns $2.50 per share. Firm C is very leveraged (risky capital structure) and earns $3.50 per share. Assume also that because of firm A's conservative financing, the market gives it a price-earnings ratio of 12; that the market gives firm B a price-earnings ratio of 10; and that the market gives firm C a ratio of 8 because of its high risk. Then, A shares would sell at $24, B shares at $25 and C shares at $24. Thus, firm B might be presumed to have the optimal capital structure of the three.

In Schwartz's general solution the amounts of both ownership capital and borrowings are considered variable and substitutable. But equity and loan capital are not considered perfect substitutes because increasing risk makes the price of borrowing rise as external funds replace owner ship funds. He shows that given the amount of equity and knowing the supply of external funds function, as well as the marginal return of earnings on assets function, one can determine the appropriate amount of borrowing, the amount of total assets and the ratio of equity to debt, which decreases for each successive amount of ownership capital. Therefore, the problem becomes one of determining the optimum amount of ownership capital.

Within this context, the important consideration is the rate of return per unit of equity capital, and this is obtained by dividing the total profit (determinate for each capital structure) by the appropriate amount of ownership capital. Thus Schwartz derives another curve (specific for each firm) whose explicit coordinates are the rate of return on equity capital and the absolute amount of equity capital.

This curve indirectly accounts for risk. As the amount of equity capital increases in a particular firm's capital structure, the debt-equity ratio and the amount of financial risk decrease. The rate of return is presented as a function of the amount of ownership capital, and the amount of ownership capital is an inverse index of risk unique for each firm.

Figure 1 shows graphically the solution proposed by Schwartz.

Let us posit a particular market indifference function representing a choice between profits and more stock (less risk) for a given type of firm. Then the rate- of-return function for a particular firm can be superimposed on this surface. The maximum that will be paid in the market for this stock is shown (in the figure) at the point of tangency, E, where the marginal rate of substitution between profit and the risk in the capital structure of this firm is equal to the marginal choice between risk and profit among the investors in the market. This is, of course, the point of tangency between the rate-of-return function and the market indifference surface. Past point E toward the right, the investors feel that any reduction in the risk of the capital structure does not compensate for the marginal loss in the rate of profits; toward the left, the investors feel that any rise in profits is not worth the additional risk assumed in the financial structure.[10]

Schwartz freely admits limitations in his model, particularly in that practically all the discussion deals with static situations. Nevertheless, his hypothesis illustrates very well the traditional view that there is an optimum capital structure, therefore a minimum cost of capital, and that this optimum structure varies for firms in different industries because the typical asset structures and the stability of earnings determine different inherent risks

---

[10] <u>Idem</u>, p. 33.

FIGURE 1

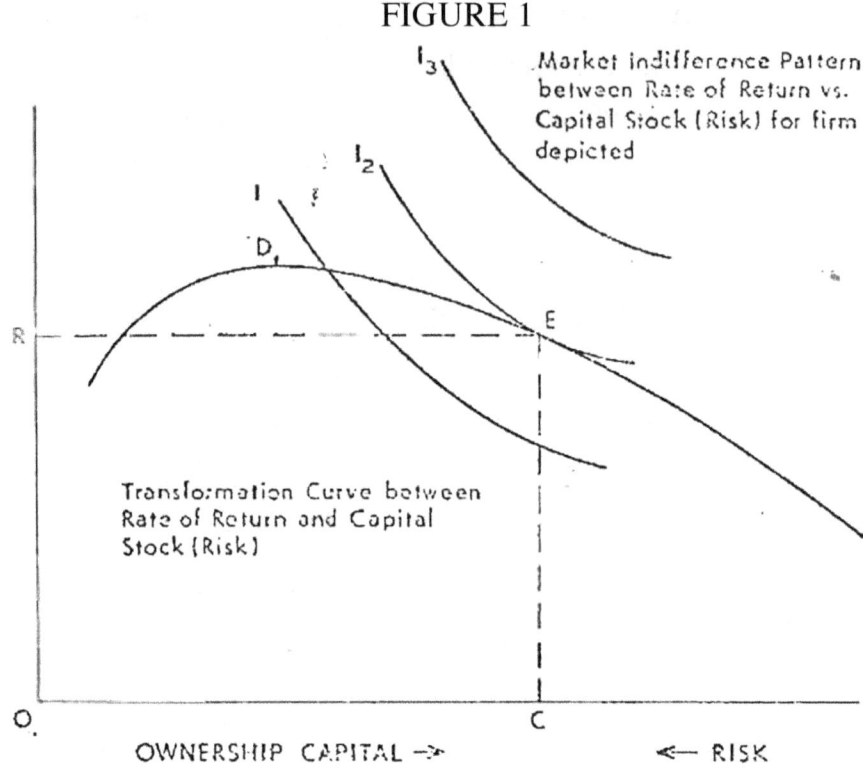

Market indifference Pattern between Rate of Return vs. Capital Stock (Risk) for firm depicted

Transformation Curve between Rate of Return and Capital Stock (Risk)

OWNERSHIP CAPITAL →   ← RISK

for different types of production.

To obtain a solution, Schwartz had to postulate a particular market indifference function, which might be impossible to determine in the real world. But he assumes that in practice, the optimal capital structure would be found by successive approximations until the best position is bracketed in.

In a recent article, E. Schwartz and J. R. Aronson[11] provide statistical evidence supporting the hypothesis that the various industries have developed optimal financial structures subject to their operational risks and to the characteristics of the industry

---

[11] E. Schwartz and J. R. Aronson, "Some Surrogative Evidence in Support of the Concept of Optimal Financial Structure," J. of Finance, XXII (1), 1967, pp. 10-17.

asset structure. In this study they define financial structure as including short-term debt and feel that this broader concept is the more relevant measure of financial risk because of the high degree of substitutability between long and short-term debt.

Part I of the study examines the financial structures of four industries (railroads, electric and gas utilities, mining and industrials) at two points in time, 1961 and 1928. The statistical tests indicate that firms in the same industry generally have similar financial structures, and firms in different industries generally have different financial structures.

Part II examines the financial structures of the industries over a forty-year period, 1923-1962. The data reveal a remarkable overall stability in the financial structures over time. Structural changes in the economy and changes in tax levels have sharpened rather than blurred the differences between the industries.

The Schwartz and Aronson findings confirm previous results obtained by Merton H. Miller[12] and contradict those obtained by A. W. Sametz,[13] who suggests that the composition of neither equity nor debt finance has been secularly stable.

---

[12] M. H. Miller, "The Corporation Income Tax and Corporate Financial Policies," <u>Stabilization Policies</u>, CMC Supporting Papers (Englewood Cliffs, N.J.: Prentice-Hall, Inc., 1963), p. 426.

[13] A. W. Sametz, "Trends in Volume and Composition of Equity Finance," <u>J. of Finance</u>, XIX (3), Sept. 1964, pp. 450-470.

Chapter IV

The Cost Of Capital In The Traditional Hypothesis

I n a broad sense, the two sources of capital for the firm are
debt and equity. In the traditional hypothesis, the cost of capital is the weighted average of the cost of debt and equity.

The Cost of Debt

A large assortment of legal instruments and contractual variations characterize the acquisition of debt capital, but the whole
process might be reduced to the determination of an interest
rate.[14] The magnitude of the cost of capital would be affected
by the interest rate on debt as well as by the proportion of debt
in the capital structure.

The question of who or what determines interest rates on the
national scale is being discussed. Two extreme views illustrate
the arguments: that the government controls the rates and that
market conditions control the rates.

---

[14] A. J. Boness, "A Pedagogic Note on the Cost of Capital," J. of Finance, XIX (1),
1964, pp. 99-106.

Government officials promote the first view. Responding to voiced concern over high interest rates and prices, President Johnson announced a new program of fiscal restraints on September 8, 1966. He called for a sixteen- month suspension of the investment tax credit on machinery and equipment, a similar suspension of accelerated depreciation methods for buildings and structures, and a three billion reduction in Federal spending out of appropriations for fiscal 1967. On September 9, 1966, the President sent a directive to departments and agencies asking them to cut back on Federal lending and borrowing activities and the Treasury announced that it would curtail public sales of Federal agency issues and participation certificates to relieve pressures on the money market. These directives carry substantial weight as indicated by the following:

By establishing a number of agencies, the Government has entered the business of banking and finance. The following are a group of these Federal agencies, which, in 1961, had loans outstanding of $27 billion.

Export-Import Bank
Commodity Credit Corporation
Banks for Cooperatives
Federal Intermediate Credit Banks
Federal National Mortgage Association
Farmers Home Administration
Public Housing Administration
Rural Electrification Administration
International Cooperation Administration

Housing and Home Finance Agency
Veteran's Administration

Not all of these credit agencies lend money—some of them merely guarantee loans or deposits made by private lenders. Each is designed to reduce the difficulty of obtaining credit in a particular field—by placing the credit of the government behind that of the borrower.[15]

President Johnson expressed his view with more clarity in his 1967 State of the Union message:

Most interest rates have retreated from their earlier peaks. More money now seems to be available. Given the cooperation of the Federal Reserve System, which I so earnestly seek, I am confident that this movement can continue. I pledge the American people that I will do everything in a President's power to lower interest rates and to ease money in this country.[16]

On June 13, 1967, the President signed the restoration of the investment credit because the original objectives were accomplished.

---

[15] M. A. Robinson, H. C. Morton, and J. D. Calder- wood, <u>An Introduction to Economic Reasoning</u> (Garden City, N.Y.: Anchor Books, Doubleday & Co., 1962 , originally published by The Brookings Institution), p. 276.

[16] State of the Union, delivered January 10, 1967, <u>U.S. Code Congressional and Administrative News</u> (St. Paul, Minn.: West Publishing Co., February 5, 1967), p. 12.

The opposing view may be expressed as follows:

Interest rates, of course, respond to market forces.[17]

The ability of a central bank to control interest rates for a time, if this be its overriding objective, is beyond dispute... The questions raised here relate instead to a less extreme monetary policy of adjusting interest rates up and down according to intuitive notions of the appropriate degree of ease or tightness in money markets.[18]

The empirical evidence brought forth by City Bank is shown in a scatter diagram where virtually no relations exist between monetary growth and interest rate changes.

It does not matter if the government achieves its objective of directly influencing interest rates or if it actually dislocates the economy with its attempts to control them. In any case the "prime rate" cannot be influenced by the firm. The firm confronts a prevailing rate which depends on factors other than the firm and the only thing a firm can do to lower its debt cost is to meet its obligations to pay faithfully, and to forecast interest rate fluctuations.

In this context, refunding is contracting one debt to replace another and as such is a consequence of interest rate fluctuations. Whenever refunding, the marginal problem is to maintain the

---

[17] First National City Bank, <u>Monthly Economic Letter,</u> New York, 1967, p. 21.

[18] Idem, p. 63.

firm's assets and earning power so that the firm's position will permit a new borrowing at the proper time.

The Cost of Equity

It is recognized[19] [20] [21] [22] that to determine the cost of capital, it is necessary to analyze how the market values the common stock. Security analysts tend to evaluate stock in terms of both dividend and earnings yields, with qualifications, based on experience and judgment, about growth rates and risks. The literature reviewed attempts to measure factors influencing capitalization rates hoping that more accurate and consistent results would be obtained, mainly for predictive purposes.

There is general agreement that the cost of equity is the capitalization rate of equity holders, the interest rate at which expected gains equal the present sum invested. The agreement stops there. The literature contains abundant, divergent and authoritative opinion as to what determines the gains expected, a vital point to make a useful estimate of the capitalization rate.

---

[19] H. Bierman and S. Smidt, The Capital Budgeting Decision (New York: The Macmillan Co., 1966), p. 144.

[20] E. E. Nemmers, Managerial Economics: Text and Cases (New York: John Wiley & Sons, Inc., 1962), p. 380.

[21] P. Hunt, C. M. Williams, and G. Donaldson, Basic Business Finance (Homewood, Ill.: Richard D. Irwin, Inc., 1961), p. 423.

[22] R. Lindsay and A. W. Sametz, Financial Management: An Analytical Approach (Homewood, Ill.: Richard D. Irwin, Inc., 1963), p. 143.

Two schools of thought are well defined: that the capitalization rate is a function of dividends and that the capitalization rate is a function of retained earnings.

A Function of Dividends

Let's introduce the first school with the popular model developed by Gordon and Shapiro.[23] They postulate that the objective of the firm is to maximize the value of the stockholder's equity. Then, define the capitalization rate of an asset as the rate of discount that equates the asset's expected future payments with its price. The only payments received by a share of stock are dividends. Thus, the capitalization rate is a function of dividends. They recognize, by their definition of capitalization rate, that what would be capitalized is a stream of future dividends. By stream of future dividends they mean an estimate derivable from known data in an objective manner, by reasonable methods, and which can be used to obtain a measure of the rate of profit implicit in the expectation. They derive the estimate by assuming the firm retains a fraction <u>b</u> of its income after tax and that the firm is expected to earn a return <u>r</u> on the book value of its common equity. Therefore, the expected stream of future dividends, would be

$$D_t = (1-b)Y_t$$

---

[23] M. J. Gordon and E. Shapiro, "Capital Equipment Analysis: The Required Rate of Profit," <u>Management Science,</u> III (October 1956), pp. 102-110.

where Y_t equals the firm's income per share of common after taxes at time t. The income per share at time t is the income at (t-1) plus r percent of the income at (t-1) retained, or

$$Y_t = Y_{t-1} + rbY_{t-1}$$

which is a compound interest expression showing the growth of the corporation's income caused by re-investing retained earnings.

After several mathematical manipulations, the resulting model is

$$k = \frac{D_o}{P_o} + g$$

which means that the rate of profit, k, at which a share of common sells equals the current dividend, D_o, divided by the current price, P_o, plus the dividend growth rate, g.

Other authorities[24] [25] [26] [27] [28] feel like Gordon and Shapiro about the importance of dividends. This school of thought does not ignore the importance of earnings, on the contrary, they are believed important because dividends are a fraction of earnings. The view is that if two similar firms with equal earnings paid different dividends, the one with greater dividends would sell

---

[24] J. B. Williams, The Theory of Investment Value (Cambridge, Mass.: Harvard University Press, 1938), p. 83.

[25] H. Bierman, L. E. Fourahr, and R. K. Jaedicke, Quantitative Analysis for Business Decisions (Homewood, Ill.: Richard D. Irwin, Inc., 1961), p. 128.

[26] H. Bierman and S. Smidt, Idem, p. 145.

[27] M. J. Gordon, The Investment, Financing and Valuation of the Corporation (Homewood, Ill.: Richard D. Irwin, Inc., 1962), Chapter 4.

[28] J. Lintner, "Optimal Dividends and Corporate Growth Under Uncertainty," The Quarterly Journal of Economics , LXXVIII (1), 1964, pp. 49-95.

its shares at a higher price,[29] or conversely, the capitalization rate (cost) of its equity would be lower. An expected increase in dividends would be reflected in an increase in the value of the shares. Thus, the equity holder gains are received through the dividend payment plus the appreciation of capital.

A Function of Retained Earnings

The second school, that the capitalization rate is a function of retained earnings, also has support.[30] [31] The rationale of this approach is that investors should be indifferent if the present value of the additional future returns resulting from earnings retention equals the amount of foregone dividends. By investing retained earnings, the increase in present value (market price) is obtained as capital gain instead of as dividend, thus a tax advantage exists which lowers the rate of return required on corporate investment for the shareholder indifference point between dividends and retained earnings.

With the market emphasis on growth, and the presumed close relationship between growth and earnings retention in the minds of investors it would not seem probable that one dollar of retained earnings should be valued low relative to one dollar of dividend. This unprobability seems supported by several

---

[29] G. E. MacDougal, "Investing in a Dividend Boost," Harvard Business Review, July-August 1967, pp. 87-92.

[30] E. Solomon, "Measuring a Company's Cost of Capital," J. of Business, XXVIII, 1955, pp. 240-252.

[31] J. Dean, Capital Budgeting (New York: Columbia University Press, 1951), p. 43.

surveys of shareholder opinion indicating that in fact capital gains are more desirable than dividends. Merrill Lynch[32] surveyed their customers (914,000 active customers at the end of 1967) in 1957, 1959, 1964 and 1967. Their results show that the primary investment goal of "capital appreciation" placed two-thirds or higher in every survey. In the 1967 survey, 76% of the customers put capital appreciation first while only 10% put dividends or interest first.

Friend and Puckett have noted the controversy over the relative importance of dividends and retained earnings and interpret their findings as follows:

> Our analysis suggests that there is little basis for the customary view that in the stock market generally, except for unusual growth stocks, a dollar of dividends has several times the impact on price of a dollar of retained earnings.[33]

The difference between the two schools may be reduced to an argument over whether dividends, and therefore, reinvestment rates, determine earnings, or whether earnings determine dividends.

---

[32] Merrill Lynch, Pierce, Fenner & Smith Inc., 1967 Annual Report, p. 4.

[33] I. Friend and M. Puckett, "Dividends and Stock Prices," The American Economic Review, LIV (5), 1964, pp. 656-682.

An Empty Argument

Solomon[34] has concluded that this argument is an empty one. He derives models which are exactly equivalent. The model basing the value of shares on dividends is:

$$V = \frac{D}{k_e} + \frac{b\,E_m}{k\,e}$$

and in terms of earnings is:

$$V = \frac{E}{k_e} + \frac{bE\,(m-1)}{k_e}$$

Where V = The value of the firm

   D = Dividend

   b = A proportionality constant, smaller than unity, which equates E to the investment allowed by new investment opportunities yielding r return.

   E = The level of (constant) net earnings expected from existing assets, without further new investments.

   k_e = Equity holders capitalization rate

   m = A proportionality constant, larger than unity, which equates the capitalization rate to the rate of return of new investment opportunities of the firm, r.

That these two equations are equivalent is shown by Solomon as follows:

---

[34] E. Solomon, The Theory of Financial Management (New York: Columbia University Press, 1965), p. 60.

... postulate the market value V of an all-equity company as the capitalized value V (at the rate k_e) of three component forms of returns. These are:

E = the level of (constant) net earnings expected from existing assets, without further net investments

G = the gross present value of capital gains expected from specific opportunities to invest funds at higher than normal rates of return

R = the reinvestment of net earnings required to achieve G.

As before, we assume a completely debt-free company. Also, we assume that all present and future investments are homogeneous as far as quality of yield is concerned, and that the level of uncertainty they involve is reflected in the capitalization rate k_e.

Let each of the investment opportunities we have postulated provide a rate of return equal to r which is higher than k_e, specifically that $r = mk_e$ where m is larger than unity. Assume that these opportunities allow us to invest R dollars a year at these lucrative rates of return and that $R = bE$ where b is any positive fraction smaller than unity.

The value of G can be computed as follows: The first investment of bE dollars yields a stream of added earnings equal to bEr dollars. The same thing happens each succeeding year. Each of these streams has a present value, as of the year it starts to flow, of bEr/k_e. This is simply the value of the constant perpetual stream discounted at the rate appropriate to its quality. What we have then is a series of investments, each of which has a gross present value equal to bEr/k_e at the time it is made. All of them together have a present value as of today of $(bEr/k_e)/k_e$ or bEr/k_e^2. Thus we have $G = bEr/k_e^2$, or, since we have put $r = mk_e$

$$G = \frac{bEmk_e}{k_e^2} = \frac{bEm}{k_e} \qquad (5.1)$$

However, in order to exploit the investment opportunities that add a gross present worth of G to the company, we must invest bE dollars each year. The present worth of these inputs is bE/k_e and so we can say that the net present worth represented by the investment opportunities is:

$$G - \frac{bE}{k_e} \text{ or } \frac{bEm}{k_e} - \frac{bE}{k_e} \qquad (5.2)$$

Having measured the net contribution of the foreseeable investment opportunities we can now measure the total value of the company. This is given by adding the capitalized value of the constant earnings stream expected from existing assets to the capitalized value of the expected investment opportunities. Doing this, we have

$$V = \frac{E}{k_e} + \frac{bEm}{k_e} - \frac{bE}{k_e} \qquad (5.3)$$

Our final equation can be stated in several ways. Combining the first and third elements, we have

$$V = \frac{E(1-b)}{k_e} + \frac{bEm,}{k_e} \qquad (5.4)$$

Since b is equal to the proportion of earnings retained and reinvested, $E(1-b)$ is equal to the dividend payout from the constant stream, and so we have a dividend and capital gains version of valuation, which can be stated as

$$V = \frac{D}{k_e} + \frac{bEm}{k_e} \quad (5.5)$$

Alternatively, we can state the model entirely in terms of net earnings data:

$$V = \frac{E}{k_e} + \frac{bE(m-1)}{k_e} \quad (5.6)$$

Miller and Modigliani[35][36] have also considered the problem of what is it that the market "really" capitalizes? In their literature review they found four distinct approaches to the valuation of shares: (1) the discounted cash flow approach; (2) the current earnings plus future investment opportunities approach; (3) the stream of dividends approach; and (4) the stream of earnings approach. They then proceed to show that these approaches are, in fact, equivalent, thus agreeing with Solomon that the argument is an empty one. The Miller and Modigliani developments exclude market imperfections, noting that what counts, from the standpoint of dividend policy, is not imperfection per se but only imperfection leading an investor to have a systematic preference as between a dollar of current dividends and a dollar of current capital gains.

---

[35] M. H. Miller and F. Modigliani, "Dividend Policy, Growth, and the Valuation of Shares," J. of Business, XXXIV (4), 1961, pp. 411-433.

[36] F. Modigliani and M. H. Miller, "Some Estimates of the Cost of Capital to the Electric Utility Industry, 1954-57," The American Economic Review, LVI (June 1966), pp. 333-391.

The following chapter is an exposition of the Modigliani-Miller hypothesis on the cost of capital, corporation finance and the theory of investment, presented in their classic 1959 paper. The article cited in this chapter appeared in 1961. It may be interesting to note that in this later article Miller and Modigliani fix upon the market discount rate as the proper cost of capital. They have thus abandoned the identification of the market discount rate with current earnings yield, in the absence of debt, which provided the decision rule in their earlier paper. In the presence of growth opportunities, they agree with traditional theory, that the relevant cost of capital is greater than the current earnings yield.

Eli Schwartz[37] has objected to the Miller- Modigliani proposition that dividend policy is neutral with respect to the market value of the firm because they ignore the special characteristics of the corporation as an economic institution.

---

[37] E. Schwartz, "A Note on the Cost of Capital, Leverage, Dividends and the Corporate Veil," The Southern Economic Journal, XXXI (1), 1964, pp. 58-61.

Chapter V

The Modigliani-Miller Hypothesis

This chapter examines the premises and conclusions of the Modigliani and Miller model.[38] It attempts to show the central place occupied by the assumption that investors consider personal leverage as an efficient substitute for corporate leverage. Then it considers the premises supporting this assumption, compares this hypothesis with the traditional viewpoint and examines some consequences which should occur under certain extreme conditions.

Before proceeding, three points should be mentioned:

1. It is most difficult to gather conclusive statistical data to resolve the arguments, and doubt exists that it can ever be done. So many factors bear concurrently on the market value of debt and equity that it is almost impossible to make final pronouncements on the effect of leverage alone. Realistic comparisons would be limited to a few similar firms, and such small samples may not be representative of the universe of firms. The definition

---

[38] F. Modigliani and M. H. Miller, "The Cost of Capital, Corporation Finance and the Theory of Investment," The American Economic Review, XLVIII (3), 1958, pp. 261-297.

itself of equivalent return classes, although conceptually evident, operationally may equate firms very dissimilar in field of activity. Conversely, it differentiates between firms in the same field: a large oil company would not be in the same class as a small oil company; a profitable rail road would not be in the same class as an unprofitable railroad. Therefore, this work deals mainly with reasoned opinions.

2. It is undisputed that when tax effects are considered, debt is advantageous, in principle. Modigliani and Miller concede this point[39] and show that arbitrage will make values within any class a function not only of expected after tax returns, but of the tax rate and the degree of leverage. Therefore, they recognize, the tax advantages of debt financing are somewhat greater than they originally suggested and to this extent, the quantitative difference between the valuations implied by their position and by the traditional view is narrowed. The dispute is not whether debt is or is not advantageous, but how much debt can be used to advantage.

3. If inflation exists, it is also undisputed that debt is advantageous, provided the firm sustains its gross income in real terms. The real income available is automatically increased as the burden of servicing debt capital falls. During long inflationary periods either the interest rate on new debt issues rises to compensate for the expected

---

[39] F. Modigliani and M. H. Miller, "Corporate Income Taxes and the Cost of Capital: A Correction," The American Economic Review, LIII (3), 1963, pp. 433-442.

rate of inflation, or the supply of debt capital contracts. Frequently these two situations occur simultaneously. But this cannot prevent firms with debt capital from benefiting substantially on existing debt until these changes occur. A firm benefits from lower cost of servicing debt until all its existing debt is repaid, a process which might take twenty-five years or more. Also, even when such changes in debt costs do occur, they tend to be both too little and too late.[40]

The Framework

Consider the framework within which the Modigliani and Miller model operates. The firm is assumed to maximize its present market value, which helps to improve the basis for a practical definition of the cost of capital. Instead of industry classification, a new term is defined: the equivalent return class. Firms in an equivalent return class are treated much in the same way that traditionalists treat industry classifications. All outputs and inputs, except those handled by the model, are assumed given.

Within this framework, Modigliani and Miller established three propositions. Proposition I states that in equilibrium:

---

[40] M. Bronfenbeuner and F. D. Holzman, "Survey of Inflation Theory," The American Economic Review, LIII (4), 1963, pp. 593-661.

The market value of any firm is independent of its capital structure and is given by capitalizing its expected return at the rate p_k appropriate to its class.[41]

$$V_J = (S_J + D_J) = {X_J}/{p_k}$$

where: J is any firm

X_J is the expected return on the assets owned by firm J.

D_J is the market value of the debts of the firm.

S_J is the market value of the common shares.

$V_J = S_J + D_J$ is the market value of the firm.

p_k is a constant capitalization rate for any firm in the equivalent return class k.

Thus, the concepts of class and of perfect correlation of expected income per share among members of the class, are central to the argument.

Proposition II states that

The expected yield of a share of stock is equal to the appropriate capitalization rate p_k for a pure equity stream in the class, plus a premium related to financial risk equal to the debt-to-equity ratio times the spread between p_k and r.[42]

$$i_J = p_k + (p_k - r){D_J}/{S_J}$$

where: i_j is the expected yield of a share of stock of the firm J.

r is the capitalization rate for safe streams.

Proposition III derives from I and II:

---

[41] F. Modigliani and M. H. Miller, "The Cost of Capital, Corporation Finance and the Theory of Investment," The American Economic Review, XLVIII (3), 1958, p. 268.

[42] Idem, p. 271.

The cut-off point for investment in the firm will in all cases be p_k, and will be completely unaffected by the type of security used to finance the investment.[43]

This chapter considers mainly the first proposition and looks at the other ones when it is convenient to clarify some point in the first. Proposition I rests on the assumption that personal leverage is an adequate substitute for corporate leverage. Personal leverage consists in that the investor buys the unlevered securities of firm A by borrowing for his personal account instead of buying securities of the levered firm B, both firms in an equivalent return class. Therefore, Modigliani and Miller do not explicitly dispute the advantage of leverage but only the value to the firm of leveraging itself since investors are assumed equally capable of leveraging themselves. They also assume that individual investors find it attractive to lever themselves and that personal leverage exists in sufficient scale.

Propositions II and III derive from Proposition I so directly that all the propositions must be accepted or rejected together.

The Operation

Modigliani and Miller explain the operation of personal leverage through arbitrage. Assuming that the market value of a firm depends on the capitalization rate applied to its class and the expected amount of earnings, then as the firm increases its proportion of debt in its capital structure, the capitalization rate

---

[43] Idem, p. 288.

for the shares rises in direct proportion to the increase in risk to the common from leverage. The increase in earnings per share of common is exactly offset by the increase in the capitalization rate for the common shares. Therefore, the levered firm cannot increase its market value per dollar earned over the unlevered firm. This central premise for the model depends on the financial environment allowing investors effective freedom to use personal leverage.

This formulation leads to belief that if levered firms reached a premium in the market over unlevered firms, both in the same class, rational investors would profit by buying the relatively undervalued securities of the unlevered firms. To buy these relatively undervalued securities, investors would leverage their personal accounts to whatever degree they preferred. These actions would restore the equilibrium of the market values and the average cost of capital for the firms. In contrast, traditionalists claim that if the firm can borrow, it will be cheaper to raise capital through debt than through new equity issues as long as the debt to net worth ratio does not go beyond the critical point. In other words, the market value of the firm is greater for the levered than for the unlevered firm, both of the same class.

Traditionalists claim that leverage does not increase significantly the financial risk to shareholder's earnings, as long as it remains confined within a certain range of the debt to net worth ratio. This is the same as saying that within this range the investor's capitalization rate is constant. Since the capitalization rate is constant while the return to the equity increases by virtue of the leverage, the price of the common stock increases and, therefore, total market value increases.

The result is that the average cost of capital to the firm declines with increases in leverage while leverage is confined within the accepted range. If the preceding holds true, one might conclude that either investors really do not believe their risks from leverage increase within the appropriate leverage range or investors are not as rational as the Modigliani and Miller hypothesis requires, or personal leverage is not really an efficient substitute for corporate leverage. F. J. Weston summarily denies that personal leverage operates as postulated by Modigliani and Miller:

> The proof depends upon the assumption that an individual who takes stocks with high leverage to a financial institution can borrow to a smaller extent than can persons who take stocks in unlevered companies to use as security for borrowing. This obviously and patently is not in accordance with the facts of business life.[44]

Traditionalists concede an increase in capitalization rate after a critical debt to net worth ratio is exceeded. They may even concede that the capitalization rate rises with increases in leverage even within the range below the critical debt to net worth ratio, but even if it does rise (within this range), the

---

[44] F. J. Weston, "The Management of Corporate Capital: A Review Article," J. of Business, April 1961, p. 135.

rising rate is not sufficient to offset the value of the increase in equity earnings. Therefore, the cost of capital to the firm declines within the tolerable range of leverage. What sparks the controversy is the claim—supported by well-reasoned mathematical formulations—by Modigliani and Miller that not only the capitalization rate is not constant for any change in leverage but that the capitalization rate change exactly offsets the value of the increase in equity earnings.

The logic of Modigliani and Miller is sound and has not been challenged. Their conclusions follow smoothly from the premises they have set up. It is the reasonableness of the premises that has been quickly subject to criticism.

> We question the validity of the theory because it is dependent upon the unsupported assumption that investors have available certain arbitrage opportunities. These opportunities in fact are not available.[45]

> This paper will expose the difficulties of justifying Proposition I for real corporations in a world where arbitrage is usually impossible, where substitutes for arbitrage are restrained and risky, and where stocks rarely sell at book value.[46]

---

[45] J. R. Rose, "The Cost of Capital, Corporation Finance and the Theory of Investment: Comment," The American Economic Review, XLIX (4), 1959, p. 638.

[46] D. Durand, Idem, p. 640.

Modigliani and Miller have attempted to answer to their most serious challengers:

If home-made leverage were as poor a substitute for corporate leverage as Durand and traditional doctrines (by implication) suggest, then levered companies would command a substantial premium in the market at least over some not insignificant range of capital structures. "Noise" in the data, of course, may well obscure this premium in particular samples; but if the cost advantages of (permanent) corporate borrowing were as large as traditional discussions suggest, they could and would be detected. All we can say is that so far they haven't been detected;...[47]

The Premises

It might be possible to determine whether or not personal leverage can perform efficiently the role that Modigliani and Miller claim for it, by considering the premises on which the assumption of personal leverage rests. If these are "obviously and patently...not in accordance with the facts of business life" or if they simply "are not available," it should not be expected that personal leverage will work exactly as the Modigliani and Miller hypothesis needs.

These are the premises:

---

[47] Idem, "Reply," p. 657.

1. The highest value (goal) pursued by investors is the maximization of their present worth (represented by their securities portfolios).
2. Investors are rational. They are willing and able to define equivalent return classes and classify firms into these homogeneous classes.
3. Personal leverage is a perfect substitute for corporate leverage. By "rolling his own" leverage through personal borrowing against the collateral of the stock, investors obtain equivalent risk-return combinations of individual and corporate leverage.
4. Capital markets are sufficiently perfect.

The first premise is acceptable. It may be argued that in the real world present worth maximization is not always pursued. As long as these deviations are infrequent and not correlated with leverage, the model would not be harmed.

The second premise is also acceptable. It is true that out of the millions of investors in the world, many might not be rational. Yet, what counts is not the number but the weight of the investors.

Strong objections exist to the third premise: that personal leverage is a perfect substitute for corporate leverage. Modigliani and Miller claim that "The exchange would, therefore, be advantageous to the investor quite independently of his attitudes toward risk."[48] They then proceed, by way of proof, with a numerical example. Their arithmetic is correct, but what

---

[48] F. Modigliani and M. H. Miller, op. cit., p. 269.

needs proof is the statement "quite independently of his attitudes toward risk."

J. Lintner comments:

> While the pro-forma funds position and the expected value and variance of the income after interest are indeed the same, the risk position of the investor carrying his own debt is, in general, inherently less favorable than if the company does the borrowing, since the variance of price fluctuations involves him in the risk of losing both his original equity investment and the amount borrowed on its collateral. Even if the probability of the occurrence of loss is the same the conditional loss is greater because of limited liability.[49]

The difference in riskiness to investors of corporate leverage as opposed to personal leverage may be emphasized by considering the risk to two investors who buy variable, but otherwise analogous earnings streams. One investor buys through personal borrowing (personal leverage), the other through a cash transaction (corporate leverage). The investor engaged in personal leverage pledges his stock as collateral. His debt is an unlimited personal liability. With the borrowed funds he buys unlevered stock representing a claim to the earnings of a firm.

---

[49] J. Lintner, "Dividends, Earnings, Leverage, Stock Prices and the Supply of Capital to Corporations," The Review of Economics and Statistics, XLIV (3), 1962, p. 265.

The second investor purchases an equivalent earnings stream from a levered firm without borrowing for his personal account, therefore, his personal liability is less. The creditor-debtor relationship between an investor and his creditor is not the same as between a corporation and its creditor. This obvious difference is important to the risk associated with personal as opposed to corporate leverage.

The investor using personal leverage pledges the stock he buys as collateral, the investor using corporate leverage lets the corporation pledge a collateral. While the corporation may pledge securities, often the real collateral are its physical assets. The market value of the stock is more likely to fluctuate in the short run than the physical assets of the corporation. Thus, the investor using personal leverage (margin account) can be sold out by his creditor during a period in which the investor who used the corporate credit is not forced to sell because the firm is still covering its fixed charges. It is also truth that personal leverage is more risky in that creditors are more able and willing to sell out the stock collateral of the individual than the physical assets pledged by the corporation.

D. Bodenhorn presents the difference in risk to the investor this way:

> Even if he (the investor) could get these terms, an investor might easily prefer an income stream of $200 of net operating income from a company less $50 interest for which the company is liable, to an income stream of $200 net operating income

less $50 interest for which he is personally liable, particularly since the corporation might not pay enough dividends in a poor year for the investor to meet the interest payment. The exactness of the substitutability of the two income streams is of vital importance...[50]

Consider the viewpoint of the lender. He has the opportunity to lend either to the corporation or to the individual investor. In the first case, the collateral is the physical assets of the corporation; in the second case, the collateral is stock of the corporation owned by the investor. Do both alternatives look equally risky to the lender? The risk might not look the same, in both cases, to the lender. The lender might feel that even in periods of poor profitability the corporation would do all in its power to meet its interest and debt repayment obligations. It might happen that during such periods the corporation might reduce or pass dividends, leaving the shareholder without the anticipated means to meet interest and debt repayment obligations. The lender then would sell out the collateral on a weak market. Therefore, it seems that from the lender's viewpoint a difference may exist between the risk run by a loan to the corporation and the risk run by a loan to an investor who is "rolling his own" leverage.

The preceding quotation and discussion imply that the lender accepts the total amount of stock owned by the investor as collateral for the loan and agrees to limit the liability of the investor

[50] D. Bodenhorn, "On the Problem of Capital Budgeting," <u>J. of Finance</u>, XIV (4), 1959, p. 485.

to the value of this collateral. In the real world this would be a most unusual situation. Normally, personal loans do not carry limited liability. Corporate leverage does provide investors with limited liability.

The corporate form transfers to stockholders the ability to draw on the resources of lenders. Therefore, investors using personal leverage to purchase stock of an unlevered firm, forego the opportunity to transfer some risk to others.

The tendency of the capitalization rate for expected earnings to remain unchanged within the acceptable leverage range might be explained partly by the acknowledgement by investors of the advantages inherent in the corporate form. It suggests that investors using corporate leverage can obtain a risk-return combination superior to that available through personal leverage. Modigliani and Miller recognize that "one minor qualification might be noted...the danger of something comparable to 'gamblers ruin,' " therefore they "might perhaps expect heavily levered companies to sell at a slight discount."

N. D. Baxter has stated that within the context of the Modigliani and Miller argument, excessive leverage can be expected to raise the cost of capital to the firm. He argues that when account is taken of "risk of ruin," a rising average cost of capital is perfectly consistent with rational arbitrage operations.

> If bankruptcy (insolvency) occurs, the debt holders, can force the firm into receivership and attempt to gain control of the corporation. If such a transition could occur without in any way

disrupting the activities of the business firm—
its revenues or its costs—there would be little
presumption that the value of the firm (or the
cost of capital) would be influenced by the risk
of ruin. To be sure, management changes would
occur which might alter the fortunes of the firm,
but in the main, the total worth of firm B (levered)
could not differ significantly from that of firm
A-(unlevered). If, on the other hand, bankruptcy
involves substantial administrative expenses and
other costs, and causes a significant decline in the
sales and earnings of the firm in receivership, the
total value of the levered firm can be expected to
be less than that of the all equity company.[51]

Consider now the fourth premise (capital markets are sufficiently perfect). This means that a market environment exists
in which one might expect the investor, confronted with equal
risk from individual and corporate leverage, to be indifferent
as to which method he uses, aside from consideration of the
relative prices of the securities. This market is characterized by
atomistic demand and supply conditions. Atomistic conditions
should prevail in the market to assure competitive prices. If
competitive prices cannot be assured, personal leverage cannot
be a perfect substitute for corporate leverage. Therefore, consider whether, on the demand side, investors—personal and

---

[51] N. D. Baxter, "Leverage, Risk of Ruin and the Cost of Capital," J. of Finance, XXII (3), 1967, p. 397.

incorporated—have equal access to the market. And on the supply side, do restrictions exist on the amount of securities supplied by the corporation?

On the demand side: Do individual investors and corporations have equal access to the capital market? Given existing conditions in the economy, the borrower's ability to pay interest and amortization determines whether or not the loan is made and influences heavily the interest rate charged. Therefore, usually the size, history and product diversification of the large corporation permit it to borrow at lower cost than individual investors.

Modigliani and Miller probably recognize that corporations usually may borrow at lower rates than individuals. But their hypothesis requires that individuals and corporations be able to borrow at the same rates, under given economic circumstances, therefore, they suggest the investor pledge as security the shares of the corporation. This technique, they apparently hope, would make the individual investor just as credit-worthy as the corporation whose shares are pledged. Institutional regulations complicate the situation, forbidding investors to borrow but a fraction of the value of the stock purchased and possibly changing margin requirements as general conditions change. Corporations are not so institutionally hindered for debt acquisition. Also, stock market fluctuations may trigger margin requirements inconveniencing the investor. Thus, in practice, individual investors and corporations do not have equal access to the market.

S. E. Seager has gathered empirical data about the historical use of borrowed funds along with equity funds to meet the total capital needs of the firm. Specifically, he compares the distribution of leverage ratios today with those of earlier periods, back to 1860 for railroads and 1900 for other industries.

> The conclusion, on the basis of the historical record of leverage ratios for firms in several industries, is that individual leverage is a partial (but not close) substitute for corporate leverage. By levering, the firm can move the investor to a preferred position that the investor cannot secure for himself through individual leverage.[52]

On the supply side: The problem of maximum and minimum debt limits is elusive. Defining the amount of bonds (meaning debt under any financial instrument) to be issued is a management prerogative exercised in very different ways from firm to firm.

J. B. Cohen and S. M. Robbins have this to say about limits on debt:

> How far to go down the debt path is a crucial question. Various benchmarks and tests have been developed. Three approaches may be distinguished: the capitalization standard, the

---

[52] S. E. Seager, "Leverage and the Cost of Capital," National Banking Review, III (June 1966), p. 507.

earnings coverage standard and the cash adequacy standard. While debt policy is usually decided at the top of the management ladder and therefore tends to be conservative, generally the approach may not be formalized. In some companies debt policy may depend on what institutional lenders or financial intermediaries (such as investment bankers) advise is acceptable and 'normal.' Or the company may make a study of what the practices are of other companies in its industry and strive to achieve an industry average or 'norm.' Or it may subscribe to the widely accepted notion, described by one authority as 'financial folklore,' that there is an appropriate limit or cut-off to long-term debt as a percentage of total capitalization. And there are some firms which adhere to tradition and simply follow time-honored practices.[53]

Modigliani and Miller imply that management would supply bonds and shares in a fashion that would suit the investors needs to be able to arbitrage.

The point of this argument is that the market value of the levered firm may be influenced by forces that do not operate on the unlevered firm. Therefore, the assumption of competitive market price for securities of levered and unlevered firms, both in the same class, may not be realistic.

---

[53] J. B. Cohen and S. M. Robbins, The Financial Manager: Basic Aspects of Financial Administration (New York: Harper & Row, Publishers, 1966), p. 585.

Another institutional force operates in the capital market: the legal lists. Regulated intermediaries are frequently restricted to investments in bonds, or to severely limited equity investments.

One last comment on the restrictions existing on the supply side of the market: the minimum bond issue. If the bond issue is going to be reasonably priced, it must have a market, and to have a market the issue must be over some minimum size. If it were below this minimum, it would have to be privately placed, at a higher cost. Thus, the supply of securities by the corporation might not be unrestricted, as required by the Modigliani and Miller formulation.

Conclusions about the Premises

Some premises postulated by Modigliani and Miller may not hold in the real world. Therefore, their reasoning should be rejected, not because of illogic or mathematical error—neither are present in their argument—but because the validity of some of their premises is doubtful.

One doubtful premise is that personal leverage is a perfect substitute for corporate leverage because:
- To borrow for a personal account may be more risky than letting the corporation borrow.
- To lend to an individual account may be more risky than to lend to a corporation.
- Investors using personal leverage forego the opportunity to transfer some risk to others.

Another doubtful premise is that capital markets are sufficiently perfect because of the action of institutional regulations and behavior.

The Tests

J. F. Weston has sought to test Modigliani and Miller's propositions by further empirical analysis. He confined his tests to the electrical utility industry because it is more homogeneous than the group of 42 oil companies, also used by Modigliani and Miller.

Weston broadened his study to include these two variables: size of the firms and their earnings growth rate. He concludes that:

> The apparent overwhelming empirical support of the generality of the Modigliani and Miller propositions rests upon measuring the gross influences of leverage and growth and attributing all the influence to leverage. When the influence of growth is isolated, the net influence of leverage on the cost of capital is found to be consistent with traditional business finance theory, rather than with the Modigliani and Miller propositions.[54]

---

[54] J. F. Weston, "A Test of the Cost of Capital Propositions," The Southern Economic Journal, XXX (2), 1963, p. 112.

Alexander Barges[55] has also examined the problems of measuring the relationship between the cost of capital and the capital structure. He indicates that where stock yield is regressed on the ratio of debt to equity, the errors introduced by sample heterogeneity with respect to riskiness and size are not random if equity is measured in terms of market value. Therefore, he suggests, the positive relationship between stock yields and debt-equity ratios found by Modigliani and Miller must be coincidental to some degree. Barges proposes to avoid these problems by running the regressions in terms of book values instead of market values. These regressions would test Proposition II insofar as the only question asked is whether or not there is a positive relationship between stock yield and debt-equity ratios, but not what is the size of the relationship. Barges looked at three industry samples: railroads, cement and department stores. He found that the evidence for a positive relationship between stock yield and leverage tends to disappear when measuring in terms of book values.

Barges also tested Proposition I and found that his regressions, on the sample of Class I railroads, between the average cost of funds and the ratio of debt to total value of the firm are negatively related.

He also points out that Modigliani and Miller defined interest payments in current terms while payments to equity are defined in terms of expected value. Therefore, the Modigliani-Miller

---

[55] A. Barges, <u>The Effect of Capital Structure on the Cost of Capital: A Test and Evaluation of the Modigliani and Miller Propositions</u> (Englewood Cliffs, N.J.: Prentice-Hall, Inc., 1963).

model does not deal with expectations of change in accepted risks, and in price expectations.

Barges' main conclusion is that the Modigliani- Miller propositions rest on a given set of assumptions about risk preference. But, he notes, the arbitrage process may require an extension of the scale of the investor's holdings, therefore, a difference may exist in the risks of the portfolios before and after arbitrage. This observation applies to the case where the value of the levered firm is greater than the value of an otherwise identical unlevered firm.

Barges also claims that the Modigliani-Miller propositions are overdeterminate. His reason is that they postulate a set of discount rates judged by the market to be compensatory for different degrees of risk. But Proposition II also specifies a relationship between returns of different risk classes that is apparently independent of the postulated set of discount rates. Yet, there is nothing to insure the consistency between the returns appropriate according to Proposition II and according to the postulated set of discount rates for the various risk classes.

To summarize, Barges feels that traditional hypotheses agree better with the observed data than the Modigliani- Miller hypotheses.

D. E. Brewer and J. B. Michaelson[56] have questioned the feasibility of the Modigliani-Miller tests. According to them, these tests are based on Modigliani-Miller's beliefs about the

---

[56] D. E. Brewer and J. B. Michaelsen, "The Cost of Capital, Corporation Finance, and the Theory of Investment: Comment," The American Economic Review, LV (3), 1965, pp. 516-524

implications of the traditional and their hypotheses about the following two relationships:

1. That between the expected yield on a firm's shares and its debt-equity ratio, and
2. That between the weighted average of the expected yields on a firm's shares and bonds and its debt-equity ratio.

Brewer and Michaelsen attempt to show that these implications differ in important respects from what Modigliani-Miller supposed them to be, and that even when appropriate corrections are made, doubt remains as to whether either view can be contradicted by the data. They advance two reasons for the latter statement: First, that the forms of the relationship between the weighted average cost of capital and debt-equity ratios are similar for both views under the tax. Second, that the tax provides an incentive for rational managers to use debt. Therefore, maximizing behavior is likely to lead to similar debt-equity ratios for all firms in the same risk class and the relationship between debt-equity ratios so the average cost of capital may be extremely difficult to estimate from the behavior of firms in a given risk class.

Modigliani and Miller[57] find it hard to take seriously the claim by Brewer and Michaelsen about having disclosed new and intractable difficulties for empirical testing. They assert that such discrepancies as would exist between their valuations and those of Brewer and Michaelsen would be substantial only at

---

[57] Idem, "Reply," pp. 524-527.

leverage levels higher than any normally observed. Modigliani and Miller note that if one looks only at the tax subsidy to debt in their model (or the "gains" from leverage under the traditional model) then one might expect every firm in the class to have the same debt ratio and that it would be as large as the tax laws or creditor restrictions permit. In the real world, however, such tight clustering does not seem to occur; and the differences in capital structure in most industries cannot be convincingly accounted for by measurement errors or risk class mixing. Therefore, empirical research should not stop.

Doubtful Corollaries

The empirical evidence shown by Modigliani and Miller consists of two samples: 43 public utilities and 42 oil companies. Their statistical analysis intends to discover relationships between the weighted average cost of capital and leverage, and between the yield on equity and leverage measured as the ratio of market value of debt to market value of equity. These are Propositions I and II which are intimately tied together.

The evidence shown might be interpreted two ways: to satisfy either the Modigliani and Miller or the traditional hypotheses.

The finding is that the curve relating the cost of capital to leverage is horizontal instead of U-shaped. Thus, Modigliani and Miller claim, "the average cost of capital with a given class k...should tend to have the same value p_k independently of the degree of leverage." On the other hand, the traditionalists look at the same curve and claim that it confirms that an optional range of leverage does exist, that all companies are operating within it, and that the horizontal curve represents the locus of optimal points.[58]

The other finding is that the yield on equity increases with leverage. Thus, Modigliani and Miller claim, "the empirical evidence we have reviewed seems to be broadly consistent with our model..." The traditionalists look at the same curve and explain it in traditional terms as follows: Assume two identical firms are organized with the same leverage. Later one firm proves to be less profitable and has poorer expectations. Therefore, its equity value falls and offers a higher yield. If the statistical analysis were made at this stage using the criterion of market value of debt to market value of equity, the less profitable firm appears to be highly leveraged and the analysis would appear to show a correlation between yield on equity and leverage.

A remarkable investor behavior is proposed by Modigliani and Miller. They propose that the average cost of capital is constant for any leverage which means, therefore, that leverage cannot become excessive. E. Solomon comments:

> ... Modigliani and Miller do not accept the fact that excessive leverage can ever cause the cost of capital function k_o to turn upwards. Their argument is that k_o remains constant with increasing leverage even if Δk_i exceeds k_e. This means that k_e falls as leverage is increased in order to maintain k_o

---

[58] E. Solomon, <u>The Theory of Financial Management</u> (New York: Columbia University Press, 1965) , p. 109.

constant. In other words, their hypothesis requires us to believe that k_e does fall, i.e., that rational investors will value a more uncertain flow of net earnings (in the more levered situation) more highly than they value a less uncertain flow from the less levered situation.[59]

Modigliani and Miller recognize explicitly this requirement of their hypothesis, "Beyond some high level of leverage, depending on the exact form of the interest function, the yield may even start to fall." What they do not recognize is that this behavior is improper for rational investors.

---

[59] Idem, p. 110.

Chapter VI

Other Hypotheses

The traditional and the Modigliani-Miller hypotheses may be contrasted algebraically as follows, in the absence of taxes:

Traditional	Modigliani-Miller
$\dfrac{X_j}{V_j} = p_k - \dfrac{(p_k - r)D_j}{V_j}$	$\dfrac{X}{V_j} - p_k$
$i_j = \dfrac{NI}{S_j} = P_k$	$i_j = \dfrac{NI}{S_j} = p_k + \dfrac{(p_k - r)D_j}{S_j}$

where: j is any firm

X_j is the expected return on the assets owned by firm j, or its net operating income. $X_j = NI + D_j r$

V_j is the market value of all of the firm's permanent capital, and $V_j = S_j + D_j$

D_j is the market value of the firm's debt

i_j is the expected yield of a share of stock in the firm j

NI is net income, the average annual value of the payments expected by common shareholders.

S_j is the market value of the common shares

r is the capitalization rate for safe streams, the interest rate on debt

p_k is the capitalization rate for X_j and for NI, of an unlevered firm in this risk class.

In words, the traditional view, in a tax-free world and without stock or bonds issue costs, may be expressed as follows: The present worth of existing shareholders will be maintained as long as new projects financed with equity raise the stock value by the amount of the investment, and as long as new projects financed with debt do not reduce shareholder's net income. It would seem to follow that the cost of capital for equity financed projects is P_j. while that for debt-financed projects is r. But this is not so because:

— substitution of debt for equity within the debt limit raises the value of the firm and increases shareholder's present worth.

— given a debt limit, no debt is available without equity.

— each addition to equity provides a base for an addition to debt.

Therefore, there should be some optimum mix of financing available in general for all projects and which firm's generally approximate striving to serve their shareholders. Accepting this, the correct cost of capital is the rate that rejects projects which do not increase shareholder's wealth. This rate will be the weighted average of and r, when the weights are the market value ratios of equity and debt to total capital, at optimum capital structure.[60]

The basic Modigliani-Miller hypothesis for a world with the same assumptions is that since the market value of the firm must rise by the amount of the investment in a new project to

---

[60] G. E. Fleischer, "Investment and Financial Decisions," The Engineering Economist, IX (3), 1964, pp. 25-45.

maintain the present worth of existing shareholders, and since the increments in net operating income associated with a new project will be capitalized at P_j, regardless of how the project is financed, it follows that a project returning less than P_k will decrease the shareholder's present worth.

Richard L. Carson[61] takes issue with Modigliani and Miller's view that the marginal cost of capital is independent of the means of investment financing. He develops his position in two parts; first, he argues that investors in stocks and bonds are buyers and sellers of its future earnings. The size of these earnings is uncertain, but for each investor it has some expected average annual value, in the probabilistic sense. The value may vary among rational investors because two investors may have different expectations even if they use the same data. Therefore, without arbitrage in predictable directions there need not be a market force tending to equate the marginal cost of capital to a given firm for all the various different kinds of financing.

Second, Carson stresses the role of management. According to Modigliani and Miller the opinion of management as to what the cost of capital to the firm is, or should be, is irrelevant because investors dictate that cost in the same sense that a perfectly competitive market dictates prices to producers. But once investors are deprived of their unanimity they lose their dictatorial power and managers gain some measure of freedom in investment and financing decision making.

---

[61] R. L. Carson, "A Note on the Cost of Capital," <u>Western Economic Journal</u>, V(3), 1967, pp. 282-287.

Carson reasons that if the cost of capital were entirely independent of the financing means, management would not be expected to exhibit any particular bias in choosing financing means, except such bias induced by tax laws. While these laws should favor debt over equity financing, by and large firms prefer to use internal funds, as shown by his study with 23 major Belgian firms. Therefore he favors the contending view as advanced by James S. Duesenberry:[62] that the firm finds retained earnings to be the lowest cost source of capital, that as the opportunity cost of foregoing dividend payments rises, debt becomes profitable, and that as the debt-to-equity ratio rises, equity issues become the cheapest form of capital.

The traditional hypothesis, in Carson's opinion, is one implication of the Duesenberry cost of capital schedule, where the optimal debt to equity ratio is obtained and maintained.

A. A. Robicheck and S. C. Myers,[63] in discussing the Modigliani and Miller hypothesis, suggested that it may be unreal because it assumes that business risk does not vary with capital structure. Robicheck and Myers suggest that possible interruption of re-investment opportunities caused by the payment of fixed charges might increase the risk of a levered firm over an unlevered firm. Thus, they implied that the existence of optimum capital structures is caused not by imperfections in

[62] J. S. Duesenberry, Business Cycles and Economic Growth (New York: McGraw-Hill, 1960), Chapter 5.

[63] A. A. Robicheck and S. C. Myers, Optimal Financing Decisions ("Prentice-Hall Foundations of Finance Series"; Englewood Cliffs, N.J.: Prentice-Hall, Inc., 1965), pp. 42-44.

the capital market but by the relationship between business risk and capital structure.

Several authors have attempted to conciliate the traditional and the Modigliani-Miller hypotheses and still others have proposed new hypotheses.

A Conciliation Attempt

A. James Boness[64] states that the propositions of Modigliani and Miller are internally consistent and are also consistent with traditional theory, though not necessarily with all partly empirical, partly theoretical traditions. Boness' statement is based on interpreting the financial risk in the Modigliani and Miller argument as the risk undertaken by a lender that his loan may be defaulted. He distinguishes between implicit and explicit lending rates. The implicit rate being required by the lender when no risk of default exists, the explicit rate required when risk by default exists. The difference between both rates is a sort of risk premium, dependent only on the proposed project and unrelated to the lender's attitude toward risk.

His argument is limited to a world that abstracts from the risk attitudes of investors, market imperfections, taxes and growth.

Boness derives a weighted average cost of capital formulation where the interest on debt is the implicit rate:

$$(1) \quad r^* = \left(\frac{D}{D+E}\right) r_d + \left(\frac{E}{D+E}\right) r_e$$

---

[64] A. J. Boness, "A Pedagogic Note on the Cost of Capital," J. of Finance, XIX(1), 1964, pp. 99-106.

where: r* represents the rate of return on the project, determined by the technology of the firm and prices in the firm's markets.

D is the debt.

E is the equity.

r_d is the implicit rate of interest on debt.

r_e is the rate of return to equity.

Then, he transforms Modigliani and Miller's Proposition II into the same form as the weighted average cost of capital, thus concluding that they are equivalent, and wonders whether the resistance to the Modigliani and Miller hypothesis lies in a confusion between the point of view of management and that of the investors.

> To the manager, r_d and r_e are given in the capital markets. The cost of capital of existing assets, r*, is given by the technology of the industry and the prices in markets in which the firm deals. But r* can be influenced by management to the extent that it elects to invest in new and different kinds of assets. The primary discretionary variables to management are D and E, or the capital structure of the firm. To investors, D, E, and r* are given and the discretionary variables are r_d and r_e, the value of either of which determines the value of the other by the constraint of equation (1) above.

A New Approach

In general, the problems of maximizing common shares present value has been approached on the basis of developing one equation in which there could be one independent and one dependent variable, everything else assumed given. E. M. Lerner and W. T. Carleton[65][66] have suggested that this approach is too limited. They propose instead to use multiple equation models able to handle multiple unknowns simultaneously. Using this approach they have attempted to integrate existing capital budgeting and stock valuation hypotheses into one generalized theory.

Lerner and Carleton constructed a two equation model. One is a valuation function, the other an investment opportunities function.

The valuation function is based on formulations developed by J. B. Williams and popularized by M. J. Gordon, where the return to investors in unlevered companies is a growing stream of dividends for an infinite period. In this model dividends grow at constant rate because the firm is assumed to earn a constant return on its assets and to reinvest a constant percentage of its earnings. This is the form of the valuation model:

$$(1.4'') \qquad\qquad P = \frac{(1-b)rA}{k-rb}$$

where: P is the price of a common share

---

[65] E. M. Lerner and W. T. Carleton, "The Integration of Capital Budgeting and Stock Valuation," The American Economic Review, LIV (5), 1964, pp. 683-702.

[66] E. M. Lerner and W. T. Carleton, "Financing Decisions of the Firm," J. of Finance, XXI (May 1966), pp. 202-214.

b is the constant earnings retention rate of return expected by investors

r is the investor's expected rate of return obtained by the firm

A is the total assets of the firm k is the market discount rate.

k is the market discount rate

This model specifies the optimal earnings retention rate, which is a proxy for the firm's investment budget, and the rate of return on assets. The optimal rates are those which maximize the price of a common share.

Using an algebraic variation of equation (1.4"), holding k constant and allowing r, b and P to vary, Lerner and Carleton determined a family of isoprice lines in a graph whose axes are r and b.

The model requires a definition of the permissible range of values of k, r and b. Therefore, k is defined as the function:

$$(1.6) \qquad k = \alpha + \varphi r b$$

where is the market discount rate on growthless shares and is a risk class whose values are between 0 and 1. Substituting equation (1.6) into (1.4"):

$$(1.7) \qquad P = \frac{(1-b)rA}{\alpha + \varphi r b - r b}$$

The stock valuation model deals with shareholders expectations of r and b. Next, Lerner and Carleton develop the investment-opportunities schedule, which deals with management's expected constraints on r and b. Having then two independent equations in r and P, it is possible to get a simultaneous solution for r and P given some b.

The investment-opportunities schedule is:

(2.3) $r_c = Y_0 + Y_0 Y_1 b_c$

where r_c is management's expected rate of return earned by the firm. $Y_0 \geq 0$ is the firm's average rate of return, expected by management, when retained earnings are zero.

Y_1 is the declining return associated with movement down an opportunities schedule as b increases.

b_c is the constant earnings retention rate expected by management.

The solution for an earnings retention rate that will maximize the price of a common share lies where the slopes of equations (1.7) and (2.3) are equal:

(2.6) $(\frac{\delta r}{\delta b})$ eq. 1.7 = $(\frac{\delta r}{\delta b})$ eq. 2.3

Figure 3 shows the graphical solution as presented by Lerner and Carleton, where b' is the solution value of management's decision variable. The firm has only one investment-opportunities schedule, sloping downwards, at a given moment, and faces a family of share prices, but equation (2.6) defines the location of the maximum price for share.

Lerner and Carleton conclude that in the case of Figure 3, "firms should not in general invest until $r = \frac{\alpha}{1-\varphi}$ (or equivalently until r = k)" and this statement "is admittedly at variance with traditional statements on the subject." Their conclusions are also at variance with the Modigliani-Miller hypothesis. While according to Modigliani and Miller, once the firm's risk class is identified its cost of capital is known and constant, Lerner and Carleton affirm that (for unlevered firms, as we are assuming) the cost of capital cannot be known until after its stock valuation equation is solved subject to the constraint of the LC function. (The LC function defines the investment-opportunities schedule, equation 2.3) Therefore, changes in the LC function, the investment-opportunities schedule, would change the firm's cost of capital.

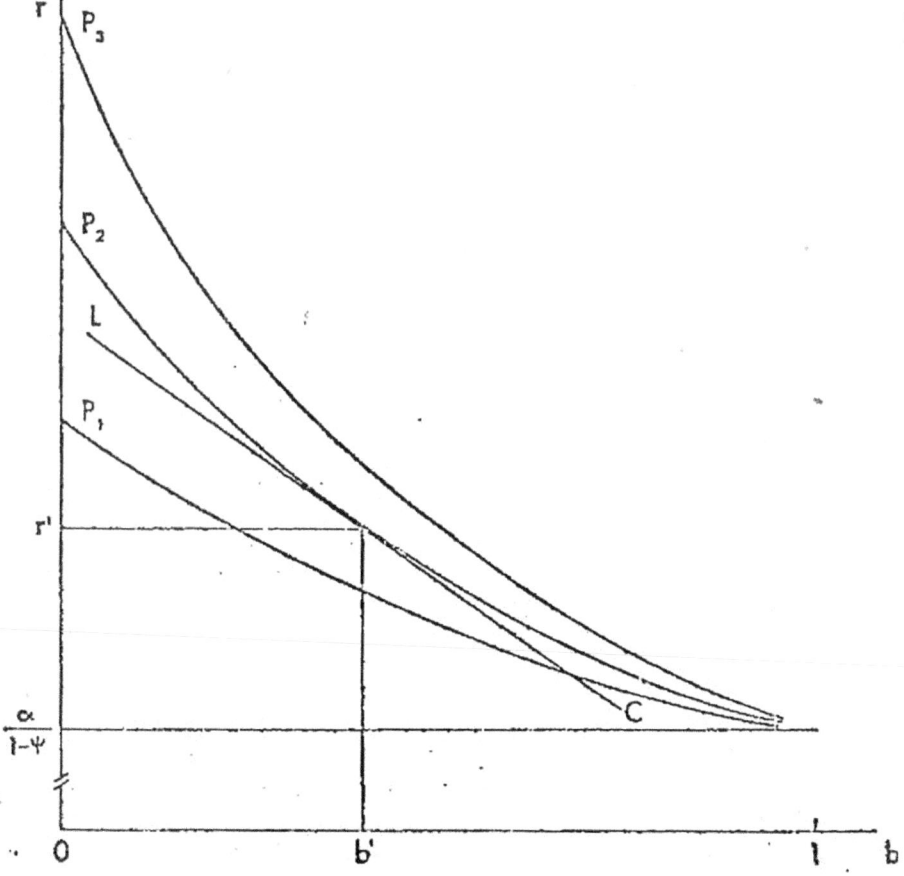

Figure 3

The hypothesis of Lerner and Carleton with respect to the cost of capital might be summarized as follows:

> ... no firm can make a rational investment decision by considering only its cost of capital schedule. Specifically, it cannot rank alternative investment projects by capitalizing the earnings stream of the project by its cost of capital. To do so implies that the solution to the problem is known before the problem is approached. Instead, a firm that is interested in maximizing shareholder wealth must determine that particular r, b combination which will maximize shareholder wealth. Once this is done and the firm's growth rate is determined, the optimum point along the cost-of- capital schedule may readily be determined.[67]

Haim Ben-Shahar and Abraham Ascher[68] as well as Jean Crockett and Irwin Friend[69] have pointed out that there seems to be an error in equation (1.4") which affects the conclusions of the model. In particular they take issue with Lerner and Carleton's conclusion that "firms should not in general invest until $r = r = \dfrac{\alpha}{1-\varphi}$ (or equivalently until r = k)."

---

[67] E. M. Lerner and W. T. Carleton, <u>A Theory of Financial Analysis</u> (New York: Harcourt, Brace & World, Inc. 1966) , p. 151.

[68] H. Ben-Shahar and A. Ascher, "The Integration of Capital Budgeting and Stock Valuation: Comment," <u>The American Economic Review</u>, LVII (1), 1967 , pp. 209-214.

[69] J. Crockett and I. Friend, <u>Idem</u>, pp. 214-219.

Ben-Shahar and Ascher emphasize that

> r in the numerator of equation 1.4", stands for
> the average rate of return on existing assets A
> and is, therefore, a constant...In the denominator,
> however, r represents the rate of return on the
> current capital budget b, and is, therefore, a
> variable. Since L and C do not differentiate
> between the r's in solving equation 1.4", the
> solution they obtain from 1.4" is invalid.

Crockett and Friend make the same point:

> A basic difficulty in the L & C analysis is that
> the internal rate of return (r) is used in several
> different senses which are at times inappropriate
> to the analysis.

Both pairs of critics offer appropriate corrections and show that, in fact, Lerner and Carleton's results are no longer inconsistent with the traditional hypothesis.

Lerner and Carleton reply[70] to their critics by emphasizing the narrow limitations of the model criticized: a one asset firm, the model referring to a firm's static equilibrium position, and postulating a constant growth rate as a variable. Therefore, by implication, their hypothesis is at a relatively earlier stage of

---

[70] M. Lerner and W. T. Carleton, Idem, "Reply," pp. 220-221.

development than what was suggested in the title of their paper. Nevertheless, theirs seems to be a fresh and promising approach.

Lerner and Carleton answer the issue of marginal rate of return in another context:

If growth is defined as the product r and b, and we ask how does growth vary with b we find

$$(1) \qquad \frac{\delta g}{\delta b} = r + \frac{d_r}{d_b} b$$

The first term on the right, r, our critics call the direct effect of the marginal rate of return; the second term, the indirect effect.

Our profit opportunities constraint (which we referred to as the LC function in our article) was specified as:

$$(2) \qquad r = Y_0 + Y_1 b$$

Obviously, if Y_0 of equation (2) corresponds to r of equation (1) and Y_1 of equation (2) to dr/db, our r is $\frac{\delta g}{\delta db}$. That is, the "marginal rate of return" or marginal growth rate with respect to changes in b, is simply the (unique solution) rate of return on assets as a function of b.

The specific form of the LC function depends upon the way the k function is specified. Hence more information is required before we can determine the variable we want r to vary with. In the trivial case, when k is a constant, our specification $r = Y_0 + Y_1 b$ will satisfy the Valuation model. In the more specific case, when k itself is a function of the investor's alternatives and the riskiness of the firm, a more complicated profit opportunities schedule may be required to constrain the valuation equation.

Chapter VII

The Baumol And Malkiel Proposition

W. J. Baumol and B. G. Malkiel[71] have developed an approach to show that in practice there is an optimal capital structure for the firm and that the cost of capital may be approximated as a weighted average of the cost of the different types of capital. Their work does not attack the work of Modigliani and Miller. On the contrary, it builds on Modigliani and Miller's pioneering work, adding to it the effect of taxes and transaction costs.

Because personal leverage is a vital part of the argument, it is best to start the exposition of the Baumol- Malkiel proposition illustrating the mechanics of it as explained by Modigliani and Miller. According to them, given perfect markets, rational investors, and abstracting from taxes, two identical firms must have the same total market value regardless of leverage differences. They claim that the investor's possibility of engaging in a process akin to arbitrage ensures that corporate leverage in itself cannot change total market value. Their proof is best explained with a numerical example.

Assume two firms, A and B, levered and unlevered respectively, identical in all other respects. Their balance sheets are:

---

[71] W. J. Baumol and B. G. Malkiel, "The Firm's Optimal Debt-Equity Combination and the Cost of Capital," The Quarterly Journal of Economics, LXXX (4), 1967, pp. 547-578.

	A	B
Shares at $1.00	700	1,000
Debentures, 7%	300	– –
Net assets	1,000	1,000

Abstracting from taxes, assume their income is a $100 perpetual annuity and that all income is distributed as interest plus dividends for firm A and as dividends for B. Therefore:

	A	B
Dividends per share	$0.1128	$0.1000

Assume further that initially A and B shares sell at ten times earnings, so that the shares of A sell for $1,128 while B's sell for $1,000. Assuming that the debentures sell at par value, the total market value for both firms are:

	A
700 shares at $1.28	789.6
300 debentures at par value	300.0
Total Value	1089.6

	B
1000 shares at $1.000	1000

An investor with 100 shares of firm A would get an annual income of $11.28. He could sell his shares for $112.80, leverage himself by borrowing $48.34 (the same leverage he had through firm A, assuming he can borrow at the same rate as the firm), and purchase 161.14 shares (assume he can buy fractional shares) of firm B.

The investor would get annual dividends amounting to $16,114, from which he would pay $3,384 in interest for his loan and keep an income of $12,730, an increment of $1.45 over his former position. Therefore, rational investors, faced with this opportunity would sell firm A shares, obtain "homemade" leverage for themselves, and purchase firm B shares until the premium on firm A shares disappeared and the prices for both firms' shares would be equal,

A similar reasoning would show that if the share prices of unlevered firm B were higher than those of levered firm A, homemade leverage would also operate to equalize them. Therefore, Modigliani and Miller concluded that in equilibrium the market value of a company is independent of its leverage: S + D = V (Constant).

When Baumol and Malkiel introduce transaction costs, which were assumed zero in. the preceding development, they note that S + D would be affected by leverage and not equal a constant V. The reason is that if personal leverage does incur in transaction costs, then the purchase of more shares of firm B, and the necessary borrowing, would require more money than assumed above, the difference being the amount of the transaction costs. This difference would tend to maintain a differential in the firm A total value, for investors desiring leverage as large as that offered by A, such that the total value of A would be higher than that of B.

Optimal Financial Structure

Baumol and Malkiel use graphs to examine the factors affecting the cost of capital. Figure 1 represents the relationship between the investor's risk attitudes and their expected earnings. It intends to show that when transaction costs are considered, the firm's financial structure is relevant to the stockholder and that from his viewpoint there is an optimal financial structure.

In the figure, the horizontal axis measures expected earnings per dollar of equity, the vertical axis measures some safety index. The magnitude of the safety index varies inversely with some measure of risk. The opportunity loci lies below and to the right of a 45 degree line through the origin because y, the safety level, will always be lower than the expected earnings , except when there is no risk. If there is no risk, both will be equal.

CC' represents the opportunity locus giving the combinations of expected earnings on equity and safety levels corresponding to different leverage ratios. I_1, I_2, and I_3 are indifference curve representations of investors attitudes on risk and expected earnings.

From the viewpoint of the investor the optimal financial leverage is that existing at the point of tangency, D, between one of his indifference curves and the firm's opportunity locus. Had management decided on another leverage ratio, say E, the investor can do nothing about it and would find himself on a lower indifference curve I_3.

Assuming cost free personal leverage the investor could do something about it. He could move to any point on CC' and then proceed to his optimal point D. In this case, management's decision on leverage does not affect the investor and all capital has the same cost as far as he is concerned. This is the case of the Modigliani-Miller hypothesis.

If personal leverage incurs transaction costs, as it does in reality, he cannot move from E to CC'. Instead,

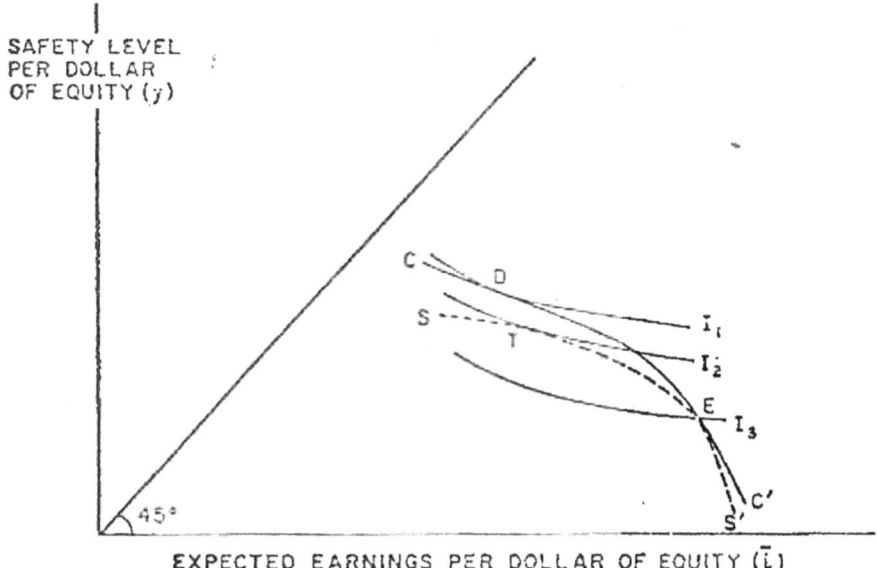

SAFETY LEVEL
PER DOLLAR
OF EQUITY (j)

EXPECTED EARNINGS PER DOLLAR OF EQUITY ($\bar{\imath}$)

Figure I

he may have available only the stockholder opportunity locus SS; which is less desirable than CC¹. It will coincide with CC' at E because no personal leverage is needed at this point, and perhaps will curve more sharply toward the axis. With any degree of personal leverage, his net earnings may be less than if the firm had chosen that leverage ratio, because the investor would reduce his expected earnings by an amount related to his transactions-cost outlay.

Therefore, the investor would at best move to the point of tangency T on SS; This would get him onto an indifference curve I_2, better than I_3 but worse than I_1. Thus, the financial structure of the firm is not irrelevant to the stockholder.

Transaction Expenses

Next Baumol and Malkiel attempt to specify the transaction expenses and other costs associated with personal leverage in the real world. From these specifications they show how to determine the optimal financial structure. They consider two cases: one where the firm's leverage is lower than what the investor desires (he wants to move toward the right in Figure 1). The other, where the firm's leverage is greater. This analysis considers different firm leverage ratios as alternative long-run choices, therefore the transaction costs involved in the personal leverage process are those of investors who are switching their holdings from cash to securities, given a leverage ratio chosen by the firm. The first part of this analysis abstracts from taxes.

When the firm's leverage is lower than what the investor desires, the investor must simultaneously purchase stocks and borrow money to increase his earnings and his risk. Normally he would start by purchasing stock on margin. His brokerage costs would be greater than otherwise would have been because he must purchase more securities than he would had the firm provided the leverage ratio he desired. In addition, the investor must pay interest on his loan, the real interest rate being significantly higher than that normally paid by the firm. After exhausting the debt load permitted by law on margin accounts, he can borrow from other sources. But now he cannot use his stocks as security for the loans, therefore, his borrowing rate is likely to rise significantly.

This analysis shows that if the investor wishes to move toward the right of the firm's decision point (Point E in Figure 1), as he must do to increase his leverage (higher expected earnings, lower safety) he will find a difference between his opportunity locus SS' and the company locus CC', with the distance between them increasing the further he gets from E. For investors whose borrowing is limited by law or custom, the individual opportunity loci SS' may fall vertically after some point. They will find an absolute limit to the extent to which they can increase their leverage via personal leveraging.

When the firm's leverage is greater than what the investor desires (he wants to move towards the left in Figure 1), he will find that personal leverage does not impose on him virtually any added transaction costs. The investor would purchase a combination of stocks and bonds instead of stocks alone, and because this does not affect the total value of his security purchases, he can do it with little change in brokerage cost. Indeed, transaction costs for bond purchases are often slightly smaller than those for common stocks. Moreover, the extent to which this process is used does not change its costs, because when the investor lends, the relevant interest rate will not vary with the magnitude of his bond purchases. In contrast, when he borrows to increase leverage, the interest rate is likely to go up with the magnitude of his borrowing. Thus, to the left of the firm's decision point, E, the firm locus EE' and the individual locus SS' correspond for a stretch. The investor buying a combination of stocks and bonds can receive precisely his pro-rata share of interest payments and earnings made by the firm. Therefore the individual opportunity locus takes the general form SS' in Figure 2.

In Figure 2 the individual locus extends a distance SC beyond the end of the firm's locus. This represents a proportion of bonds in the individual portfolio so large that its safety is greater than that provided by the firm shares in the case where firm's debt were zero (point C). Point S represents a portfolio including bonds only.

Taxes

At this point in the analysis, Baumol and Malkiel introduce tax considerations. Corporate income taxes reduce proportionately both the expected earnings and the shareholder's safety level because the safety level itself is a potential level of corporate income. More important, the difference between the firm locus CC', and the individual locus SS' increases substantially because of the different tax treatment for debt and equity and because the shareholder cannot duplicate, through personal leverage, the tax advantages available to the firm. This is so because by shifting from equity to debt, the firm can increase the total amount of interest plus dividend payments it can make.

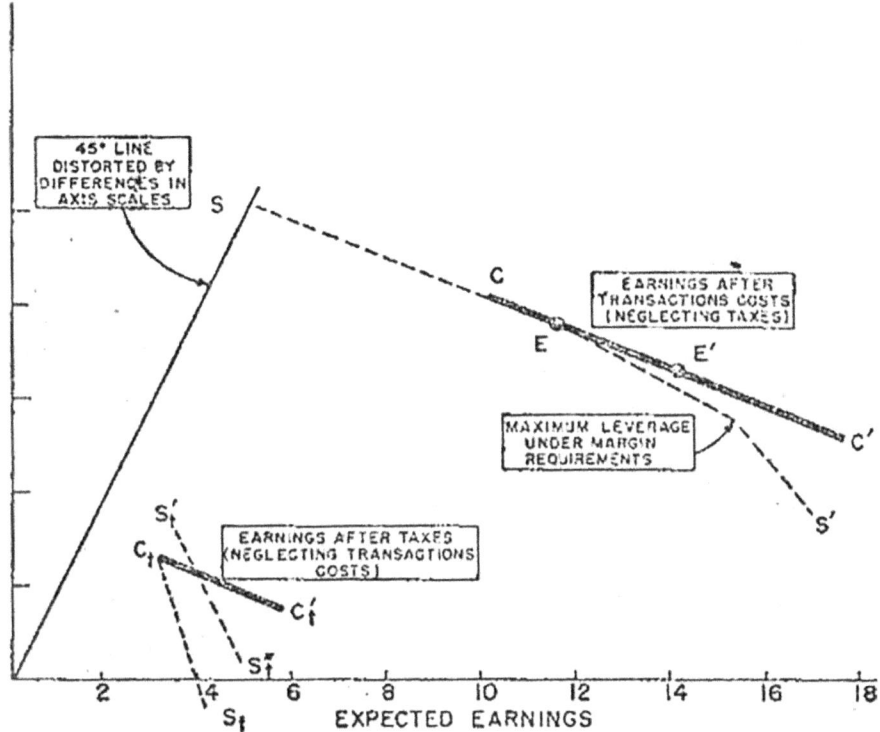

Figure II

The tax arrangement can cause the two opportunity loci to intersect as they do in the lower left-hand corner of Figure 2 (curves $C_T C_T'$ and S_T', S_T'').

The investor desiring little leverage may gain by investing in a highly levered company that gets maximum tax advantage and then purchasing sufficient bonds to undo the leverage to the extent desired.

In contrast with the Modigliani-Miller hypothesis, Figure 2 shows that, even without transaction costs personal leverage is not an effective substitute for corporate leverage. Despite the fact that Baumol and Malkiel allowed in their calculations for a tax advantage to the shareholder (some return taxed at

91

preferential capital gains rates) the shareholder cannot get by himself the same combination of return and safety that the firm can provide by alternative leverage ratios.

Relevance of Dividends

The lower portion of Figure 2 shows the asymmetric effects resulting when an individual rolls his own leverage and unmakes company leverage. If the company chooses a levered capital structure, the investor wanting no leverage is better off than he would be buying unlevered common shares directly (the relevant section of the individual opportunity locus S_T' S_T'' lies well above the company locus). If the individual makes more leverage than the firm chose, he would be worse off than he would be if he purchased common shares in a firm that had itself the desired leverage ratio. This suggests that in practice, the dividend payout ratio is relevant to the shareholder, in contrast to Modigliani and Miller. For instance, if the existing corporate leverage were below the optimal level, shareholders would be better off if dividends were increased and more debt were used to finance new investments. Thus, it would be advantageous to shareholders for the firm to borrow as much as is consistent with prudence and with legal and institutional limitations.

Marginal Costs

Once Baumol and Malkiel have shown the existence of an optimal capital structure, they consider the real marginal cost of debt and equity. Their Figure 5 shows their approach. It shows what would happen to the firm opportunity locus C_1 C_1' if it were to raise additional funds and kept them idle. This approach avoids any confusion resulting from discussing the revenues produced by the investment financed with the additional funds. Therefore, the figure takes into account only the costs of the funds.

Assume first that the firm were initially at its

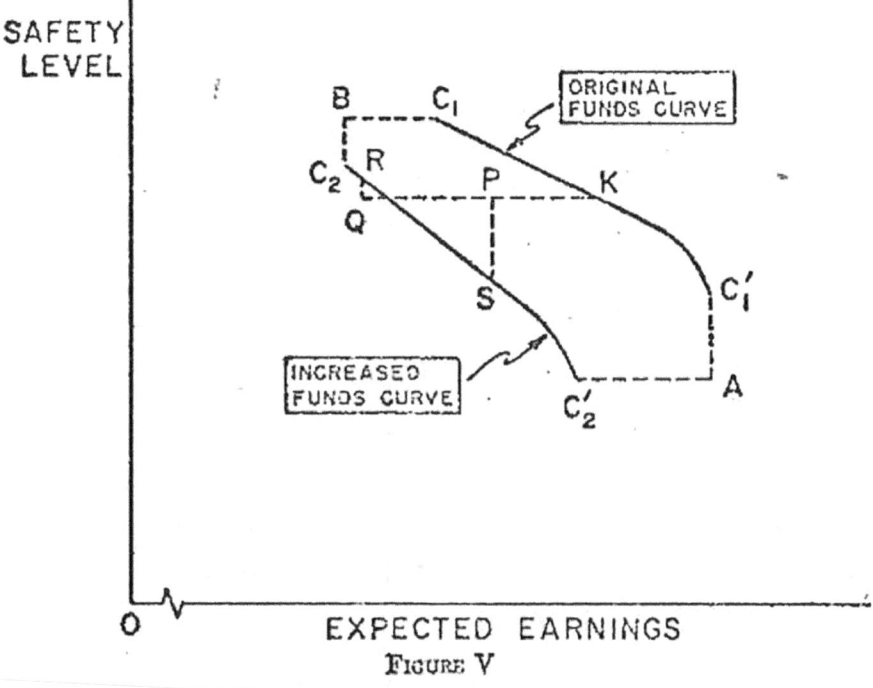

FIGURE V

all equity point C, and that it raised new equity. Ignoring possible revenues that could be obtained with the new funds, the added equity reduces the expected earnings per dollar of equity (along BC_1) because now existing earnings would be spread over more equity. Some change in the safety level (C_2B) is also likely, so that the firm would move to some new point, C_2. If the firm were starting from a highly levered position C_1' and issued new bonds, the safety level would decrease and earnings per share would be reduced, so the firm would move to a point such as C_2' Some curve $C_2\ C_2'$ would connect these extreme points and represent the opportunity locus corresponding to debt-to-equity ratios in the additional funds.

The same figure also helps to explain the difference between retained earnings and a new stock issue as means to increase equity. Assume that the shareholders of a certain firm do not need to consume the income from their holdings. The issuance of securities usually involves heavy transaction costs, which are avoided by retention. Because transaction costs can be translated into an equivalent stream of payments, they are equivalent to a long-term earnings reduction. Therefore, the curve CC' corresponding to a new stock issue will, ceteris paribus, lie below and to the left of the curve involving retained earnings. Therefore, in this case, earnings retention is an economic way to raise funds.

The alternative case is that where shareholders need to consume the income from their holdings. A policy of retention would force the shareholder to sell part of his holdings, therefore, the stockholder, instead of the firm, incurs the transaction costs. However, it is likely the retention would still be the optimal method for raising new equity because capital gains taxes are lower than those on dividend income and because the transaction costs incurred in selling new equity issues are usually larger than brokerage costs in selling shares.

Figure 5 is also useful to describe the difference between the effects of new debt and of new equity on the welfare of the shareholder. Assume that the firm's initial financial position is at point K. If it were now to increase its debt, this would reduce expected earnings by an amount KP. It would also reduce the safety level by an amount PS. Thus, the firm's position would move to a point S on the lower opportunity locus $C_2 C_2'$. It can be seen now that the real marginal cost of debt is greater than KP, the amount of interest required by the funds in question, because the indifference curve through the debt point, S, will lie below the indifference curve through the nominal-debt-cost point, P.

In the alternative case, if the firm were not to increase its equity, the expected earnings per dollar of equity would decrease by some larger amount, KQ, than it would with the issue of debt. But because the leverage ratio would be reduced there might even be an increase in safety level, QR. Therefore, the real marginal cost of equity would be lower than its nominal amount, QK.

At this point Baumol and Malkiel are ready to develop an explicit measure of cost of capital and see the effect of personal leverage on its magnitude.

The Cost of Capital

In Figure 6 they add three stockholder indifference curves to Figure 5. The first, I_1, is tangent to the older opportunity locus at initial point K, assumed optimal. The second indifference curve is tangent to the new lower opportunity locus, with optimal point E. The third indifference curve goes through point S, the increased debt point. At this stage Baumol and Malkiel define as an index of the marginal cost of capital the increment in expected earnings per dollar of equity needed to get the stockholder back to his initial level of satisfaction after the change in financing. They also assume, for the moment, taxes and transaction costs to be zero.

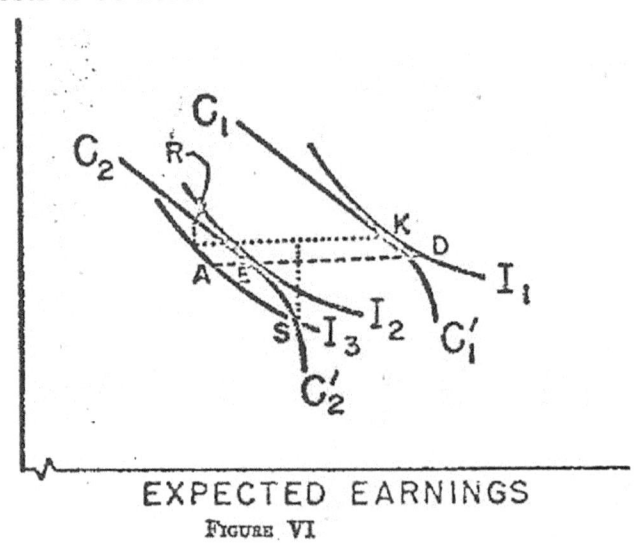

EXPECTED EARNINGS

FIGURE VI

SAFETY LEVEL

For this analysis, they consider the investor to go through a step-wise adjustment process. First, the added debt moves him from K to S. Then the investor uses personal leverage to move himself along $C_2 C_2'$ to his optimal point E. From E, an annual cash payment equivalent to an increase in expected earning ED will move him back to his initial utility level. This, then, is the incremental cost of debt capital to him. But had personal leverage, or even a partial adjustment, not been possible, so that he would have been forced to stay at point S, then he would have been on a lower indifference curve and the real incremental cost of capital (the compensating variation in earnings) would have been the larger amount AD.

Without transaction costs or taxes, the shareholder can move to optimal point E just as easily from R as from S. Thus, with personal leverage his cost of equity would also be ED. This is the Modigliani and Miller result: with costless personal leverage, the real marginal costs of debt and equity are always equal.

To introduce the effects of taxes and transaction costs, Baumol and Malkiel use Figure 7. In it, if the new financial decision point is P on $C_2 C_2'$ and P is not the optimal point, S_0', the shareholder opportunity locus will be $S_1 S_1'$, which lies below $C_2 C_2'$ to the right of point P.

SAFETY LEVEL

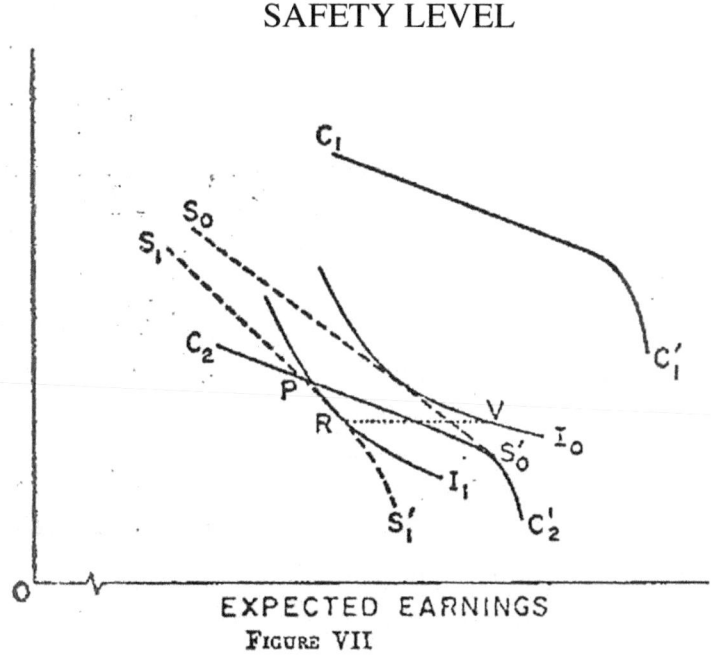

EXPECTED EARNINGS

FIGURE VII

Again, after the investor moves to point P, the best adjustment available to him involves a further move along $S_1 S_1'$ to the point of tangency, R, with his indifference Curve I_1. This is a second-best adjustment leaving him better off than he was at P, but not as well as he would have been at S_0'. Thus, there is an added real cost in acquiring capital by a nonoptimal method as compared with the no-tax, no-transaction-cost case. This added real cost may be represented by distance RV. The marginal real costs of debt and equity need no longer to be equal because the magnitude of RV varies with the location of point P.

Cost of Capital as a Weighted Average

Baumol and Malkiel's analysis attempts to conciliate an apparent contradiction between financial theory and ordinary economic analysis.

On standard economic theory, the real cost of homogeneous resources is assumed to be the cost of the cheapest source available. In the theory of corporation finance, the cost of capital is assumed to be a weighted average of the cost of capital from all sources available. Modigliani and Miller proposed that the cost of capital is , and Baumol and Malkiel show that:

$$(7) \qquad \frac{\bar{X}}{V} = \frac{(\bar{\imath} S + r D)}{S + D}$$

where: X is the expected value of future earnings before interest

V market value of the firm

expected yield on equity

r interest rate on debt

S market value of equity

D market value of debt

Equation (7) shows clearly that the cost of capital is the weighted average cost of debt and equity.

Baumol and Malkiel stress that these propositions of economic theory and corporation finance theory are not really conflictive because they apply to different matters. They point out that both r and are only nominal costs and are not real costs. The debt interest rate understates the true cost of debt because it does not allow for the leverage risk incurred by more borrowing. The expected yield on equity neglects the risk reduction resulting from lowered leverage ratio when there is a ceteris paribus increase in the amount of equity. Therefore, equation (7) is just an algorithm to translate the nominal cost of funds into their real magnitude.

With regards to whether or not the real cost of funds agrees with the economic theory proposition that one borrows only (or first) from the cheapest sources, Modigliani and Miller show that when both debt and equity are used, their real marginal costs are both given by . Therefore, when both sources are used neither has a lower marginal cost, just as economic theory requires. But because of taxes and transaction costs existing, the marginal cost of new shares may be greater than . If such is the case, new equity is more expensive than new debt or retained earnings. Baumol and Malkiel's optimal solution is a corner-solution where no new funds come from new shares, so the marginal costs of new shares will not affect the real marginal cost of capital to the firm.

The development and conclusions of this work depend heavily on the geometry of the curves used for illustration. Therefore, it should be made clear that the curves were not drawn in arbitrary manner. As Baumol and Malkiel show in their Appendixes, they are based on careful calculations involving realistic numerical examples. For instance, in Figure 2, curves CC' and SS' are based on the following assumptions:

- 1 percent commission on stock purchases
- 3/4 percent commission on bond purchases
- 5 1/2 percent interest rate on an individual's margin borrowing
- 5 percent interest rate on corporate borrowing.

Chapter VIII

Summary

I n years past, the maximization of the profit of the firm was the proposed criterion of goodness for investment decision making. It has now been abandoned generally (in the literature). The firm's profit maximization might have been convenient for economic models under certainty. Under uncertainty conditions, as is the case in the real world, the profit of the firm becomes a family of mutually exclusive outcomes described as a perhaps subjective probability distribution. Particularly when using debt, a project may increase the return on equity only at the sacrifice of increasing the variability of the outcomes.

The criterion of goodness generally accepted (in the literature) is the maximization of the present market value of existing common shares.

The specification of a criterion of goodness is important because it permits developing a rational mechanism for investment decisions. A rational mechanism for investment decisions must focus on the proper goal, have a correct method to measure the proposals, and have a valid accept-reject criterion. Most important, the goal, the measurement and the accept-reject criterion must be consistent with each other.

This rational mechanism is now available (in the literature): the goal is the maximization of the present worth of existing common shareholders, the measurement method recognizes the time value of money and the accept-reject criterion is the cost of capital.

Given this criterion of goodness, the next problem was to develop some means to predict how stock values react to decisions taken by the firm. In other words, one needs a stock valuation theory. This theory should permit predicting whether or not a given project would increase the present worth of existing shareholders.

Given that what the existing common shareholders own is equity, and that capital is also available to the firm under the form of debt, the problem becomes one of whether or not the existence and the proportion of debt in the financial structure of a firm has any effect on the return obtainable by existing common shareholders. In other words, whether or not financial structure affects the cost of capital.

The debate (in the literature) centered on the determination of the costs of debt and equity and on the interaction of these costs, because the question to be answered is: Will the investment, financed in a given manner, increase the price of the common shares? This question requires an understanding of the effect of financial structure on market valuation. To gain this understanding, historical data has been examined and from it, deductions have been made about the effect of financial structure on market values.

It has been recognized that the investor has the option, in the case of investing in levered firms, to invest in equity alone, debt alone, or in a mixture of debt and equity. Depending on the manner of his investment, the investor may obtain different combinations of risk and return.

Broadly speaking, the debate could be reduced to two viewpoints. One is that the cost of capital is not affected by financial structure and is constant for a given firm. The opposing viewpoint is that capital structure does affect the cost of capital, thus, an optimum capital structure exists with which the cost of capital is a minimum.

The first view has been best presented by Modigliani and Miller. They argued that financial structure has no effect on the cost of capital mainly because the investor, through personal leverage, can offset any decision by the firm with regards to financial structure.

The second view has been best presented by Baumol and Malkiel. They show, by using Modigliani and Miller's arbitrage model and taking into consideration transactions costs and taxes, that an optimal capital structure does exist, that the firm should borrow as much as judiciously possible and that personal leverage is not an efficient substitute for corporate leverage.

Bibliography

Abrams, F., retired chairman of the board of Standard Oil, quoted in "Have Corporations a Higher Duty than Profits?", Fortune, August 1960, p. 108.

Barges, A. The Effect of Capital Structure on the Cost of Capital; A Test and Evaluation of the Modigliani and Miller Propositions. Englewood Cliffs, N.J.: Prentice-Hall, Inc. , 1963.

Baumol, W. J., and B. G. Malkiel. "The Firm's Optimal Debt-Equity Combination and the Cost of Capital," The Quarterly Journal of Economics, LXXXI (4), 1967, pp. 547-578.

Baxter, N. D. "Leverage, Risk of Ruin and the Cost of Capital," J. of Finance, XXII (3), 1967.

Ben-Shahar, H., and A. Ascher. "The Integration of Capital Budgeting and Stock Valuation: Comment," The American Economic Review, LVII (1), 1967, pp. 209-214.

Bierman, H., L. E. Fourahr, and R. K. Jaedicke. Quantitative Analysis for Business Decisions. Homewood, Ill.: Richard D. Irwin, Inc., 1961.

_____, and S. Smidt. The Capital Budgeting Decision. New York: The Macmillan Company, 1966.

Bodenhorn, D. "On the Problem of Capital Budgeting," J. of Finance, XIV (4), 1959.

Boness, A. J. "A Pedagogic Note on the Cost of Capital," J. of Finance, XIX (1), 1964, pp. 99-106.

Brewer, D. E., and J. B. Michaelson. "The Cost of Capital, Corporation Finance, and the Theory of Investment: Comment," The American Economic Review, LV (3) , 1965, pp. 516-524.

Bronfenbeuner, M., and F. D. Holzman. "Survey of Inflation Theory," The American Economic Review, LIII (4), 1963, pp. 593-661.

Carson, R. L. "A Note on the Cost of Capital," Western Economic Journal, V (3), 1967, pp. 282-287.

Cohen, J. B., and S. M. Robbins. The Financial Manager: Basic Aspects of Financial Administration. New York: Harper & Row, Publishers, 1966.

Crockett, J., and I. Friend. "The Integration of Capital Budgeting and Stock Valuation: Comment," The American Economic Review, LVII (1), 1967, pp. 214-219.

Dean, J. Capital Budgeting. New York: Columbia University Press, 1951.

Duesenberry, J. S. Business Cycles and Economic Growth. New York: McGraw-Hill, 1960.

Durand, D. "The Cost of Capital, Corporation Finance and the Theory of Investment: Comment," The American Economic Review, XLIX (4), 1959, pp. 639-654.

_____. "Costs of Debt and Equity Funds for Business: Trends and Problems of Measurement," <u>Conference on Research in Business Finance</u>. New York: National Bureau of Economic Research, 1952.

First National City Bank, Monthly Economic Letter. New York, 1967.

Fleischer, G. E. "Investment and Financial Decisions," <u>The Engineering Economist</u>, IX (3), 1964, pp. 25- 45.

Friend, I., and M. Puckett. "Dividends and Stock Prices," <u>The American Economic Review</u>, LIV (5), 1964, pp. 656-682.

Gordon, M. J. The Investment, Financing and Valuation of the Corporation. Homewood, Ill.: Richard D. Irwin, Inc., 1962.

_____, and E. Shapiro. "Capital Equipment Analysis: The Required Rate of Profit," Management Science, III (October 1956), pp. 102-110.

Graham, B., D. L. Dodd, S. Cottle, and C. Tatham. <u>Security Analysis</u>. Fourth edition. New York: McGraw-Hill Book Company, 1962.

Guthman, H. G., and H. E. Dougall. <u>Corporate Financial Policy</u>. Englewood Cliffs, N.J.: Prentice-Hall, Inc., 1955.

Hunt, P., C. M. Williams, and G. Donaldson. <u>Basic Business Finance</u>. Homewood, Ill.: Richard D. Irwin, Inc., 1961.

Kaplan, A. D. H. <u>Big Enterprise in a Competitive System</u>. Washington, D.C.: The Brookings Institution, 1964.

Lerner, E. M., and W. T. Carleton. "Financing Decisions of the Firm," J. of Finance, XXI (May 1966), pp. 202-214.

_____. "The Integration of Capital Budgeting and Stock Valuation," The American Economic Review, LIV (5), 1964, pp. 683-702.

_____. "The Integration of Capital Budgeting and Stock Valuation: Reply," The American Economic Review, LVII (1), 1967, pp. 220-221.

_____. A Theory of Financial Analysis. New York: Harcourt, Brace & World Inc., 1966.

Lindsay, R., and A. W. Sametz. Financial Management: An Analytical Approach. Homewood, Ill.: Richard D. Irwin, Inc., 1963.

Lintner, J. "Dividends, Earnings, Leverage, Stock Prices and the Supply of Capital to Corporations," The Review of Economics and Statistics, XLIV (3), 1962.

_____. "Optimal Dividends and Corporate Growth Under Uncertainty," The Quarterly Journal of Economics, LXXVIII (1) , 1964, pp. 49-95.

MacDougal, G. E. "Investing in a Dividend Boost," Harvard Business Review, July-August 1967, pp. 87-92.

Merrill Lynch, Pierce, Fenner & Smith Inc. 1967 Annual Report.

Miller, M. H. "The Corporation Income Tax and Corporate Financial Policies," Stabilization Policies, CMC Supporting Papers. Englewood Cliffs, N.J.: Prentice-Hall, Inc., 1963.

_____, and F. Modigliani, "Dividend Policy, Growth, and the Valuation of Shares," J. of Business, XXXIV (4), 1961, pp. 411-433.

Modigliani, F., and M. H. Miller. "Corporate Income Taxes and the Cost of Capital: A Correction," The American Economic Review, LIII (3), 1963, pp. 433-442.

_____. "The Cost of Capital, Corporation Finance and the Theory of Investment," The American Economic Review, XLVIII (3), 1958, pp. 261-297.

_____. "The Cost of Capital, Corporation Finance and the Theory of Investment: Reply," The American Economic Review, XLIX (4), 1959, pp. 655-669.

_____. "The Cost of Capital, Corporation Finance and the Theory of Investment: Reply," The American Economic Review, LV (3), 1965, pp. 524-527.

_____. "Financial Policy and the Cost of Capital: Some Empirical Results." Unpublished paper read at the Econometric Society Meetings, December, 1962.

_____. "Leverage, Dividend Policy and the Cost of Capital." Unpublished paper read at the Econometric Society Meetings, December, 1960.

_____. "Some Estimates of the Cost of Capital to the Electric Utility Industry, 1954-57," The American Economic Review, LVI (June 1966), pp. 333-391.

Morris, R. The Economic Theory of Managerial Capitalism. New York: The Free Press of Glencoe, 1964.

Mumey, G. A. "Earnings Probabilities and Capital Costs," J. of Business, XL (4), 1967, pp. 450-461.

Nemmers, E. E. Managerial Economics; Text and Cases. New York: John Wiley & Sons, Inc., 1962.

Robicheck, A. A., and S. C. Myers. Optimal Financing Decisions. (Prentice-Hall Foundations of Finance Series.) Englewood Cliffs, N.J.: Prentice-Hall, Inc., 1965.

Robinson, M. A., H. C. Morton, and J. D. Calderwood. An Introduction to Economic Reasoning. Originally published by The Brookings Institution. Garden City, N.Y.: Anchor Books, Doubleday & Co., 1962.

Rose, J. R. "The Cost of Capital, Corporation Finance and the Theory of Investment: Comment," The American Economic Review, XLIX (4), 1959.

Sametz, A. W. "Trends in Volume and Composition of Equity Finance," J. of Finance, XIX (3) , Sept. 1964, pp. 450-470.

Schwartz, E. "A Note on the Cost of Capital, Leverage, Dividends and the Corporate Veil," The Southern Economic Journal, XXXI (1) , 1964, pp. 58-61.

_____. "Theory of the Capital Structure of the Firm," J. of Finance, XIV (1), 1959, pp. 18-39.

_____, and Aronson, J. R. "Some Surrogative Evidence in Support of the Concept of Optimal Financial Structure," J. of Finance, XXII (1), 1967, pp. 10-17.

Seager, S. E. "Leverage and the Cost of Capital," National Banking Review, III (June 1966), p. 507.

Solomon, E. "Measuring a Company's Cost of Capital," J. of Business, XXVIII, 1944, pp. 240-252.

_____. The Theory of Financial Management. New York: Columbia University Press, 1965.

State of the Union, delivered January 10, 1967, U.S. Code Congressional and Administrative News. St. Paul, Minn.: West Publishing Co., February 5, 1967.

Weston, J. F. "The Management of Corporate Capital: A Review Article," J. of Business, April 1961, p. 135.

_____. "A Test of the Cost of Capital Propositions," The Southern Economic Journal, XXX (2), 1963.

Williams, J. B. The Theory of Investment Value. Cambridge. Mass.: Harvard University Press, 1938.

Wippern, R. F. "A Note on the Equivalent Risk Class Assumption," The Engineering Economist, XI (3), 1966, pp. 13-22.

CPSIA information can be obtained
at www.ICGtesting.com
Printed in the USA
LVHW081233021120
670452LV00003B/194

9 781632 217240